Y0-CBQ-726

SHE HOLDS ALL THE RECORDS . . .

She has written over 60 detective novels in 55 years!

✳

She has written twelve plays, including *The Mousetrap*, the longest-running play in theatrical history!

✳

Her sales are near the 400 million mark, and she makes about $10,000 a week in royalties!

✳

She has created some of the world's most popular detectives—Hercule Poirot, Miss Marple, Tuppence and Tommy . . .

✳

In England in 1971 a mysterious poisoning case was solved because the detective had read one of her novels—ten years earlier!

✳

Who is she, this *Queen of Crime*, this *Duchess of Death*, who one critic called "a perfect hostess serving hemlock at a cocktail party"?

✳

THE MYSTERIOUS WORLD OF AGATHA CHRISTIE looks behind Agatha Christie's veil of privacy, and discovers a woman even more remarkable than her public suspects!

The Mysterious World of
AGATHA CHRISTIE

Jeffrey Feinman

Copies of this printing
distributed in the United Kingdom by
arrangement with Tandem Publishing Ltd.

AWARD BOOKS
NEW YORK

FIRST AWARD PRINTING 1975

Copyright © 1975 by Jeffrey Feinman

All rights reserved.

AWARD BOOKS are published by
Universal-Award House, Inc., a subsidiary of
Universal Publishing and Distributing Corporation,
235 East Forty-fifth Street, New York, N.Y. 10017.

Manufactured in the United States of America

Contents

The Mysterious World of
AGATHA
CHRISTIE

Chapter I

The Poison in the Case

Robert Egle was sixty years old in July 1971. He was the first to die. In November, Frederick Biggs, fifty-six, died also. The small factory town of Bovingdon, Hertfordshire, England, was panicked. Four more workers at Hadland's photographic equipment works were stricken with the same "Bovingdon Bug."

The afflicted all had the same symptoms: vomiting; a weakness in the limbs; scaling skin; hallucinations; paralysis; falling out of the hair; and then, death. After Biggs died, plant owner John Hadland called a meeting to investigate. Deliberate poisoning was not suspected. Some form of industrial pollution, perhaps.

"The thing caught my attention. She said something like '... and all her hair, to see it coming out all over the pillow. Coming out in handfuls.' And then I thought of Mary Delafontaine. Her hair came out. And I remember what you told me about that girl in Chelsea, getting her hair all pulled out in handfuls . . . it must mean something."

"Bless you," I said. "You're wonderful!"

I slammed back the receiver then took it off again. . . . "Listen," I said, "is Ginger's hair coming out by the roots in handfuls?"

"Well—as a matter of fact I believe it is. High fever, I suppose."

"Fever my foot," I said. "What Ginger's suffering from, what they've all suffered from, is. . . ."*

At the meeting in Bovingdon, one employee who had joined the firm as Egle's assistant just eleven weeks before his death spoke with encyclopedic knowledge about the effects of various poisons. Frederick Graham Young was twenty-four, an intense young man with piercing eyes and hair slicked back. He amazed the plant owner and his fellow workers with his mastery of medical terms and his knowledge of all manners of toxins. A detective from Scotland Yard

*Excerpts from *The Pale Horse*, copyright 1961 by Agatha Christie, Ltd. Published by Dodd, Mead & Company, Inc, 79 Madison Ave., New York City.

who attended the meeting was also impressed with Young.

On the day after the meeting in Bovingdon, the detective had lunch with Dr. Hugh Johnson, an eminent forensic specialist, in London. He spoke of Young's amazing knowledge and of the symptoms of the "Bovingdon Bug."

"What put thallium into your head?"

"Several things suddenly came together. The beginning of the whole business was the thing I saw that night in Chelsea. A girl whose hair was being pulled out by the roots by another girl. And she said, '*It didn't really hurt.*' It wasn't bravery, as I thought, it was simple fact. It didn't hurt.

"I read an article on thallium poisoning when I was in America. A lot of workers in a factory died one after the other. Their deaths were put down to astonishingly varied causes. Amongst them, if I remember rightly, were paratyphoid, apoplexy, alcoholic neuritis, bulbar paralysis, epilepsy, gastro-enteritis, and so on. Then there was a woman who poisoned seven people. Diagnoses included brain tumour, encephalitis, and lobar pneumonia. The symptoms vary a good deal, I understand. They may start with diarrhoea and vomiting, or there may be a stage of intoxication, again it may begin with pain in the limbs, and be put down as polyneuritis or rheumatic fever or polio—one patient was put in an iron lung. Sometimes there's pigmentation of the skin."

"You talk like a medical dictionary!"

"Naturally. I've been looking it up. But one thing always happens sooner or later. *The hair falls out.* Thallium used to be used for depilation at one time—particularly for children with ringworms. Then it was found to be dangerous. But it's occasionally given internally, but with very careful dosage going by the weight of the patient. It's mainly used nowadays for rats, I believe. It's tasteless, soluble, and easy to buy. There's only one thing: poisoning mustn't be suspected."**

Dr. Johnson remembered the two preceding passages from Agatha Christie's mystery, *The Pale Horse*, and told the detective that the symptoms he had described could be traced to thallium, a poison that had never before been used in Britain.

Informed of the nature of the "bug" and suspicious of the detailed knowledge shown by one

**op cit.
The Pale Horse.

man, the police searched Frederick Young's lodgings in a rundown Hemel Hampstead boardinghouse. They found "enough thallium to keep a pharmacy in business for an entire month."

Test tubes and bottles containing a wide range of poisons were lined up along a shelf and on the windowsill. There was a diary describing his "experiments." Each of his fellow employees was identified by a letter: "J—he is a friend, so it's out of the question." But he poisoned J. "F—he is doomed to premature decease."

In one corner of the room, police found a suede jacket with another small bottle of thallium. When Young was arrested at his father's home, a few miles away, he said, "It was my exit, but I did not have a chance to use it." He quoted lines from Oscar Wilde's *The Ballad of Reading Gaol* and confessed to the poisonings readily. He speculated that his likeness would be immortalized in Madame Tussaud's and when asked if he felt remorse, replied: "All I feel is the emptiness of my soul."

Agatha Christie described her *fictitious* poisoner in *The Pale Horse*, written a decade before the events at Bovingdon:

"Is he mad?" I asked.

"I'd say he's gone over the edge now ... it does something to you, you know. Killing people. It makes you feel powerful and larger than life. It makes you feel you're God Almighty. But you're not. You're only a nasty bit of goods that's been found out .... You scream and you rant and you boast of what you've done and how clever you are. Well, you saw him."

"Did you always suspect him ... right from the beginning?"

"Well, he would draw attention to himself," said Lejeune. "As I told him, if he'd only sat back and done nothing, we'd never have dreamed that ... [he] had anything to do with the business. But it's a funny thing, that's just what murderers can't do ... they can't let well alone. I'm sure I don't know why."**

Dame Agatha Christie was upset on hearing of the Bovingdon murders. She hoped "this fellow hadn't read her book and learned from it." But if there was any Christie that Frederick Graham Young had copied, it was John Christie, the mass murderer, one of Young's heroes.

**op cit.
   The Pale Horse.

He even knew how many layers of wallpaper had covered the kitchen walls in Christie's Rillerton Place home.

Although no one in Bovingdon, not his landlady, fellow workers, nor his employer, had any suspicion of Young's fascination with poisons, the police might eventually have caught him even without his boasting. Young's history was, to say the least, macabre.

Frederick Graham Young was sentenced, at the age of fourteen, to fifteen years in Broadmoor Mental Hospital, a maximum security institution. He had poisoned a classmate, his father, his sister, and his stepmother. His victims all survived, except his stepmother, who died—supposedly from natural causes—shortly after Young was confined. Not until he was convicted for the Bovingdon murders did Young admit that his stepmother had been his first thallium victim.

Six years before his sentence was up, hospital officials recommended Young's release, saying: "This man has suffered a deep-going personality disorder which necessitated hospitalization throughout the whole of his adolescense . . . but he was . . . of above average intelligence and capable of sustained effort. He would fit in well and not draw any attention to himself in any community." Young received a brief period of training, employment was found for him at John Hadland's, Ltd., and he was released.

Just one day after he arrived in Bovingdon, Young visited a local chemist with a letter he had forged, asking for toxins to be used in experiments at a nearby university. He got the poisons, signing the poison register with an assumed name.

Young immediately began "experimenting" with his old friend antimony, and with thallium, strychnine, and aconite tincture. He knew just how much poison to administer in his experiments so the process of death would be slowed. He visited his victims at their bedsides to commiserate and mark their progress. When the first victim of the "Bovingdon Bug" died, Young told his sister that he would get Egle's job, and he did. But Young's motive was not as mundane as just trying to get ahead. At his trial, Young claimed the motivation of the scientist: "I ceased to see them as people. They became guinea pigs." The St. Albans court sentenced him to life imprisonment.

The release of other mental patients had become more difficult since the Young case. Agatha Christie need not have worried about Young using information in her book to poison his friends. However, since Dame Agatha has always been interested in the plight of those institutionalized for mental disorders, she could well have worried about the effects of the Young case on Britain's liberal attitude toward the mentally ill.

"One case such as Young's can inflict irreparable damage on a program that has been successful for many years," said the Home Secretary. Hospital Chief Superintendent Dr. Patrick McGrath said that (usually) "When we consider release, we err on the side of caution." A prominent London psychiatrist said, "There is always the chance that the patient is even cleverer than you."

Dame Agatha could have told them about the risks in attempting to single out a potential murderer in the crowd. "Whoever my villain is," she has said, "it has to be someone I feel *could* do the murder. A murderer must have the kind of nature which doesn't have any brakes on it. I suppose vanity is very important. You couldn't have a *doubtful* murderer—all brakes are removed and he's certain of what he's doing. But this needn't be obvious to others. Especially as one gathers it very rarely in real life. In real life, when there's a murder, everyone seems so astonished. People always say about the murderer: 'He was such a charming man. So kind, so good to children.' Perhaps one day I shall meet a real one. I never have, so far as I know."

After a lifetime interest in crime, with a hundred mysteries conceived and solved, Agatha Christie had caught her first real murderer with the Young case. Testifying during the trial, Dr. Johnson admitted as much. He said that something clicked in his head when he heard the symptoms of the bug in Bovingdon. He remembered the descriptions in *The Pale Horse* and set the police on the trail. This was the first time thallium had been discovered as the instrument of death in an English poisoning case—except for the case of Dame Agatha's highly imaginative use of the toxic, ten years earlier.

And so there are at least four Englishmen who owe their very lives to Mrs. Christie's profitable preoccupation with the poison in the case. The rest of us owe her something, too.

Chapter II

The Phenomenon of Agatha Christie

Agatha Christie has made more money out of murder than any woman since Lucrezia Borgia. "Give me a nice deadly phial to play with," Agatha said, "and I'm happy." And who could doubt it? Since she published *The Mysterious Affair at Styles* in 1920, Agatha Christie has written twelve plays, numerous short story collections, and more than sixty detective novels. The precise number is vague since the lady has manuscripts that she keeps to herself for posthumous publication. Indeed, she has some that she has forgotten about completely and from time to time she runs across them tucked away in the bottom of a closet.

Her publishers have lost count of her total sales: "It's impossible to say. The thing has gotten completely out of hand." Sales probably exceed 400 million copies.

To further complicate matters, Dame Agatha has produced six romantic novels under the pseudonym of Mary Westmacott and travelogs under her married name of Agatha Christie Mallowan.

Her plays are regular smash hits on Broadway, in the West End, and the world over. Once she had three plays running simultaneously in London, two in the U.S., and a half-dozen others elsewhere, from Paris to Podunk. *Witness for the Prosecution* ran more than a year in London and in New York. *The Mousetrap*, still playing a run of more than twenty-three years in London, is the longest running play in the history of the theater anywhere in the world and has been seen by more than 1.8 million people.

Movies abound, only two of which Dame Agatha likes: *Witness for the Prosecution* and the recent *Murder on the Orient Express*. She hated the Miss Marple films because the plots were all botched up and often had nothing whatever to do with the books she had written.

The payoff is fabulous. In poor years Agatha Christie's income never drops below $5,000 weekly. Currently she tops $10,000 a week, although she will confess, "I must work because I don't know how much there is in the bank."

She never has had a head for figures, she

says, and doubts if she will ever be able to un-
ravel the mystery of her two bank accounts:
one has a lot of nasty red figures, and her
business manager won't allow her to touch the
other one. Since she has a prodigious skill for
bridge, chess, crosswords, and other intriguing
puzzles, as evidenced by her books, one would
think she could also balance her bank statement. It may be that she doesn't care to flaunt
the enormous sums of money she earns. Long
ago she began signing over her royalties to various members of her family because she knew
she would never be able to use it all and she believes that money should be enjoyed.

Despite her success, Agatha Christie has remained an enigma in the eyes of the public.
There is not another famous author alive about
whom so little is known. She refuses all interviews and photographs and permits only the
barest, most carefully monitored statements to
be released by her publishers.

She has turned down all offers, however
tempting, of lecture tours and television appearances. Her reclusiveness has been so extreme that for a long while she wouldn't even
allow her publishers to print her photograph on
her book jackets. Recently, a young college
student wrote to her requesting biographical
information for a term paper. Agatha Christie
replied: "Information or biographies, articles

about writers tell you nothing of interest—only facts. It's the actual books and stories you have to study and write about—not the persons who wrote them." Dame Agatha has written her autobiography for posthumous publication and says she will set the record straight then.

Recently, however, the public's fascination with the detective novel has had an enormous resurgence, and it is the Agatha Christies that are out in front. Added to this is the enormous success of the film *Murder on the Orient Express*. To some extent, age seems to be mellowing Dame Agatha's attitude toward the press; she is seen more and more often in the pages of fashionable magazines and making the columns of the London papers.

Nothing—neither age nor her many extracurricular activities, such as decorating houses and traveling or archeological digs—curbs her blandly maddening pen. She punctually delivers a new novel every year nicely in time for the Christmas trade. At eighty-five years of age, Dame Agatha, wounded but undaunted by a hip injury which allows her to walk with the aid of a cane, shows no signs of becoming posthumous anytime soon. Her books breeze right along with the times, employing such an *au courant* plot device as a jet plane hijacking in place of the slower detaining of the Orient Express which she used in the 1930s. But as up-to-the-minute as the new novels are, Dame Agatha clearly prevails as a representative of a vanished era.

She is a charming, gray-eyed, elderly lady who likes to indulge her passions for cooking, playing in the sunshine, and decorating houses. At one time, Dame Agatha and her husband Sir Max Mallowan owned eight houses in Britain, ranging from London townhouses to Greenway House, their magnificent country estate of the sort where high-tone murders are committed in the Poirot mysteries. "They just seemed to accumulate," says Dame Agatha. "I didn't realize there were that many until I counted them all." Lady Mallowan concurrently restored and redecorated all eight houses. Today, however, the number of Mallowan residences has dwindled to three and Dame Agatha's collecting is restricted to Victorian papier mâché trays and needlepoint.

Agatha Christie talks about reading and writing in a curiously unliterary way. "I was brought up on Dickens," she told Francis Wyndham in an interview. "Always loved him and hated Thackeray. I love Jane Austen, too. Who doesn't? With Dickens you can never really tell where the story is going. I always feel with him he got awfully tired of his characters and dragged in more—but the new ones were just as wonderful! *Bleak House* is my favorite, such a good plot. I once tried to write a film version. The numbers of characters in that book! I found I had to cut out many of the best ones.

"I read contemporary detective stories, of course. There's a very good American writer called Elizabeth Daly. Michael Gilbert's early ones were excellent—*Fear to Tread* and *Smallbones Deceased*. He writes more thrillers now, which I find less interesting. Another American, Margaret Millar, is very original. Patricia Highsmith is a good *sinister* writer. Hugh Walpole was wonderful at writing about cruelty and things like that. Otherwise I like Elizabeth Bowen, Graham Greene—you can't put him down, which after all is the real test, even though he irritates you sometimes. I enjoy Muriel Spark very much, she's always so original.

"One is very lucky to have writing as a trade. One can work hard at it but also have delicious days of leisure and idleness. Young people nowadays have no time at all for what I call leisure, thinking, and all that. They're overshadowed by education. They're so desperate that they won't get jobs unless they have degrees. At that age they should be really enjoying themselves—kicking up their heels like a filly in the fields.

"So much education tends to specialise you—

it makes you more interested in taking things in than in giving things out. Very few people really stimulate you with the things they say. And those are usually men. Men have much better brains than women, don't you think?"

That statement would lead one to believe that Agatha Christie holds a rather traditional view of the role of women in society—no feminist she. It is true that Mrs. Christie's public statements often read as though they were written for Miss Marple, a staunch believer in the old virtues. But what Dame Agatha *does* belies the traditional attitude her statement might imply. She is no dilettante, no tony patroness of the arts, no hausfrau.

With probably more money than she could spend in an additional eighty-five years, Dame Agatha works—and she works hard. She has sometimes turned out three and four books in a year for several consecutive years. For the past few years she has written only one book a year, though.

In fact, one of the greatest mysteries about a woman so surrounded with mystery is why, at this point in her life and career, she works at all. According to her agent, Edmund Cork; "There is no vanity in her makeup and certainly she doesn't need the money. She writes because the idea of giving pleasure to others appeals to a nice person."

Dame Agatha acknowledges that the task sometimes becomes tedious. "There are always moments when you get bored with the people and the plot," she explains. "Then you sit around for a few days before going back to it." She worries over the problem of how to kill her victims and usually settles upon a lethal blow with a blunt instrument rather than "very clever ways of killing people" that would be too complicated for an unsophisticated woman, as she chooses to call herself.

These are times when all the worrying in the world won't bring a plot into line, she notes. "Sometimes you get involved with a character and can't see how to manage him or her and throw them out and start again. It's like auditioning actors."

For an extremely private person like Agatha Christie, fame may bring more burdens than rewards, but she does enjoy the things her wealth makes possible. "Being a successful author means that one can take a taxi whenever one wants one," she says. Another benefit is to have servants. "My idea of bliss is to be surrounded by legions of well-trained servants," she noted.

Chapter III

The Early Years

Dame Agatha Christie (also known as The Queen of Crime and The Duchess of Death) was born Agatha Mary Clarissa Miller in Torquay (pop. 53,000), Devonshire, on September 15, 1890. Her early years were spent in the well-to-do, insular society which characterized Queen Victoria's vigorous reign.

England, particularly upper-class England, has always been noted for its eccentrics, not the least of whom was Agatha's mother. In the days when such things were not done in the "right" families, she married a wealthy American stockbroker, Frederick Alvah Miller.

An American was an oddity in the village of Torquay. Situated on the English Channel, not far from where the *Mayflower* sailed, Torquay is one of those towns around which has grown up a whole legend of English countryside. Royally favored landowners have been ensconced there since the days of the Henrys, when cheerful peasant farmers were only too happy to pay homage to the gentry. By the 19th century, Torquay had become an exclusive resort area for titled families, as well as the domicile of landed gentry. It is the setting for many of Agatha Christie's mysteries.

How Mr. Miller wheeled and dealed stocks and bonds from Devonshire has never been explained. More likely he was a gentleman of independent means. It was unusual in those days for families to live from the income of investments—gentlemen seldom went out to work. At any rate, Frederick Miller figures in his daughter's life mostly by his demise, for he passed away while Agatha was still quite small.

Agatha had an older sister; it was this first-born child who received the lion's share of Mr. Miller's affections simply by the fact that she had more years to spend with her father. Agatha herself remembers only her mother.

The family tree of Mrs. Miller has never been revealed by her daughter, but it is generally surmised that she was from an extremely wealthy, multiply-titled family. Despite the fact that she lived all her life in the English countryside, Mrs. Miller was an up-to-date young woman. A married woman of thirty or forty, even though she lived in complete leisure, was the most sophisticated woman one could meet in those days. Agatha Christie herself would later remark that women were much more interesting then. "They had good minds. They read and studied and were exceedingly interesting to talk to. Now people can often only talk about one thing." Agatha's mother was definitely one of the women to whom her daughter referred in her remark. She was abreast of all things cultural, social, and political in the world. "Mrs. Miller was the sort who cannot spot a new trend without rushing to put salt on its tail," said one journalist.

The subject which most preoccupied Mrs. Miller was how to bring up her girls. Her "whims" were usually supported by what was currently *avant garde*, but that was not necessarily what was fashionable in the rigid circles of English society. "When it was time for my sister to go to school," Agatha Christie recalls, "my mother was just at the stage of believing that children should get the very best education. So my sister went to what is now Roedean College. But when the time came for me to go, my mother's views had changed. She now believed passionately that education destroyed a child's brains and was ruinous to the eyesight. So I never went to school at all."

It was, in fact, usual in those days of Victoria and later of Edward VII for a well-brought-up young girl to lead a sheltered life in the bosom of her family. Under no circumstances did she go off to school as did her brothers. Instead, she received tutoring at home from a governess. The range of tutoring varied from family to family. For the most part, a girl's education consisted of the "graces"—music, painting, sewing, and so on. In families where intellect was prized beyond gender, a girl might learn Latin, Greek, mathematics, and history—but always at home.

Mrs. Miller's decision to send her older daughter out to school was based on a radical trend of the moment. But when it was Agatha's turn, Mr. Miller had passed away, leaving a painful gap in the family circle. It was decided to keep Agatha with her mother. Also replacing the school fad was the shocking premise that girls should be taught by their own mothers. Most families rejected that idea outright as it was well-established that governesses and tutors were responsible for the education of children, just as nannies were responsible for a child's daily care. But Agatha's mother was eager to see that her girls were not caught in the entrapments of a stodgy past. She looked forward and governed herself on the principle that the new is better than the old. Thus, Agatha was kept at home and her mother became her teacher.

In many other ways Agatha's girlhood centered on her mother far more than was usual. The old story of the nanny assuming the role of mother while the mother remained a remote and glamorous figure to the child did not exist for Agatha. Her whole world revolved around her exuberant and sympathetic mother.

Fortunately for the Miller girls, their free-wheeling mother did not believe in aimless dreaming. She took for granted that there was nothing her daughters couldn't do. When Agatha was confined to bed with a severe cold one day, Mrs. Miller encouraged her to write her first short story. "Of course you can," she told her protesting daughter. And indeed she could. Agatha was further encouraged in this pastime by a Devonshire playwright, Eden Phillpotts, who was a friend of the family. "For some years I enjoyed myself very much," says Dame Agatha, "writing stories of unrelieved gloom where most of the characters died."

The Miller girls and their mother may have been isolated in the sense that theirs was a small, quiet household, but isolation was more the rule than the exception for young girls in Victorian society. It is doubtful that Agatha spent much time feeling lonely or sorry for herself. On the contrary, she enjoyed long stretches of solitary thinking. "I still insist on being left entirely alone for a few hours every day," she says.

Agatha read fairy tales and romances in large quantities and developed a passion for Dickens as a result of listening to her mother read aloud from his works.

From an early age Agatha studied piano and later, in her teens, she received voice lessons. She equated her love of music with her attraction to Milton's *Paradise Lost*: "Of course, I didn't understand it, but I did love its sonorous sounds." Nigel Dennis, writing for *Life* magazine many years later, said that there was a sort of "musical agreeableness" in Agatha Christie's criterion even today: "Well-tempered voices and gentle manners are what she looks for in her friends and considers morally desirable, because they are usually signs of kindness, warmheartedness and civilized convictions."

Childhood endowed Agatha Christie with many other enduring attributes. Even now, at eighty-five, she prefers to work on rainy days because sunshine makes her want to be a truant and hurry out to play. She also developed a sensible amount of self-indulgence, a hostility to routine of any sort, and extreme dislike of puritanical moralizers who believe that pain and struggle are good for the soul.

Agatha was far from being a silent, introverted child. She had an unusually good and close understanding with her mother which must have made her early years happier than that of many an upper-class child. Looking at Agatha as she approached womanhood, one would have seen a quiet, attractive redhead who wanted to be an opera singer. In fact, she studied voice in Paris when she was in her teens and even made the concert platform. But her singing career, as well as her ability at the piano, never developed beyond that, probably because of an innate shyness that made performing a terrifying experience for her.

When Edward the Peacemaker died in 1910, Agatha Miller was twenty years old. The years of the Great War lay just ahead, but as yet England was unsuspecting, still secure in its position as an enormously wealthy country that ruled half the world from its island fastness. The terrible upheaval that rocked the English social structure following the war did little to alter Agatha Miller's belief that England was somehow at the center of things, a place both ordinary and, at the same time, exemplary of the human condition. This civilized view of a vanished society, which was created throughout a childhood deeply rooted in Victorian dogma, would permeate all of her future work. There is no better place for a murder than in an English country manor.

In August of 1914, on the eve of World War I, Agatha Miller married a flamboyant flying officer in the Royal Flying Corps, Colonel Archibald Christie (C.M.G., D.S.O., Order of St. Stanislaus with Swords). Colonel Christie went off directly to France and his bride set to work for the Voluntary Aid Department in her home town, qualifying as a dispenser in the hospital at Torquay. Agatha likes to say that she owes her knowledge of poisons to this experience. Her interest in medicine and psychology is common among writers—they are fascinated to know what makes things tick, especially what makes bodies tick. Agatha learned enough about poisons in the Torquay hospital to last her a lifetime.

As the war dragged on, Agatha Christie continued her hospital work and wrote stories in her spare time. It has been said that she wrote her first mystery story because of a dare. Her sister supposedly taunted her with, "I bet you can't write a good detective story." Agatha promptly sat down and wrote *The Mysterious Affair at Styles*. The dare seems more the sort of thing a twelve-year-old would throw at a six-year-old. In fact, Agatha was twenty-six at the time and her sister was thirty-two.

More likely, Agatha Christie's metamorphosis into a mystery writer was a natural development. As she herself puts it: "I suppose I was trying things, like one does. I first tried to write poetry. Then a gloomy play—about incest, I think. Then a long, involved, morbid novel—some of the writing wasn't too bad, but the whole thing was pretty poor. Then I did *Styles*. I hadn't read many detective stories—there weren't very many to read. I'd read Sherlock Holmes, of course, with passion. And a book called *The Mystery of the Yellow Room* [Leroux], translated from the French, which I thought very good. I'm afraid it reads rather peculiarly now."

Whatever prompted her, Agatha Christie was an author hungry for drama and already in the habit of killing off most of her characters. She settled herself into the detective form and worked for several months on *Styles*. Using one of the Belgian refugees who lived in Torquay as a model, she created her first detective—the foppish, waxen-moustached Hercule Poirot. Her main influences were Holmesian: "the pattern of the clue" and "the idiot friend." Her own "Watson" was Captain Hastings, an Army officer recently invalided home from the Front who served as a foil to Poirot. Hastings was as slow-witted as Poirot was clever; therefore, even if the reader could not keep up with Poirot's "little grey cells," he was still well ahead of Hastings' brain waves.

If one reads it today, it is hard to believe that *The Mysterious Affair at Styles* was turned down by a half-dozen publishers and kept by the Bodley Head for nine months before John Lane published it in 1920. *Styles* is mystery writing of the first caliber, but at that time the precepts of detective fiction were not so clearly established as they are today. *Styles* ushered in the Golden Age of mystery writing in which the detective story was purified in the form of a complex puzzle. The mazelike plot was of utmost importance and any emotional engagement between characters was minor, if it existed at all. Moulding and polishing this unique form was Agatha Christie's major contribution to the genre of mystery writing. It is true that she also displayed a gift for convincing, humorous dialogue and interesting characters in her first novel, but these alone were not enough to make her stand out from many other mystery writers of the day. It was her dazzling focus on "the game" that was original.

Christie perfected the technique of misleading the reader, switching his allegiance from one character to another, and ending up with the one person least suspected as the murderer. Her method was, and still is, to conceal nothing, to lay precisely the same things before both the reader and the detective, and to lay them out so naturally that the most innocent things are suspected of being criminal and the most criminal of being innocent. In the case of *Styles*, for example, the most obvious person to have committed the murder in fact *does* commit the murder. Christie loaded the dice so heavily against him, making him so obviously odious, that every reader discounted him halfway through, but he had done it all the same. In *The Mysterious Affair at Styles* she also displayed her fascination with and knowledge of poisons, confusing the method of murder so nicely that the reader must retrace the clues to understand how the whole thing works out in the end.

It was Holmes who said, "It is my belief, Watson ... that the lowest and vilest alleys in London do not present a more dreadful record of sin than does the smiling and beautiful countryside." Agatha Christie demonstrated just how well she could exploit the countryside which was so familiar to her. Murder takes place in the most ordinary environment; Styles, in this instance, is very much like Torquay. Country lanes and country houses continued to be Agatha's favorite sites for murder in the coming years.

The Mysterious Affair at Styles, for all its stunning assets, had only a modest sale of 2,000 copies and made 25 pounds for its author. It was not published in America until ten years after its British publication, but when Allen Lane launched his Penguin Books in 1935, *Styles* had become such a standard in the mystery lists that it was one of the earliest volumes published in this series of unusually "literary" books.

Chapter IV

The Success of Roger Ackroyd

When she sold *The Mysterious Affair at Styles* to John Lane in 1920, Agatha Christie was "transported with happiness." Until that time, she had never considered making a career for herself as a writer. Certainly she had no idea of what the future held for her. "I went on writing detective stories," she says. "I found I couldn't get out. If I'd known it was for life, I'd have chosen some rather younger detectives. God knows how old they must be by now!"

Hard on the heels of *Styles*, Agatha Christie published five new mysteries in rapid succession. *The Secret Adversary* appeared in 1922 and introduced those happily married sleuths, Tuppence and Tommy Beresford. *The Murder on the Links* was next (1923); followed by *The Man in the Brown Suit* (1924); *Poirot Investi-*

gates (1924) ; and *The Secret of the Chimneys* (1925), which introduced Superintendent Battle. *The Man in the Brown Suit* was a mystery novel with a one-time-only detective protagonist, but *The Murder on the Links* and *Poirot Investigates* once again featured Hercule Poirot, the mastermind with the egg-shaped head, the charmingly inflated ego, and a passion for neatness.

England was recovering from the war, but it was clear to everyone that English life would probably never be the same again. The Christies settled themselves into a more permanent domestic arrangement, buying a house at Sunningdale, Berkshire, which they named "Styles." After more than six years of marriage, it was their first home together. Their only child, Rosalind, had been born in 1919, and Mrs. Christie quickly adapted herself to a well-organized life of motherhood and writing.

With each new detective story her fame grew. She was not especially shy of publicity at this time; on the contrary, a double-page spread in *The Weekly Sketch* in 1923 illustrated in pictures and text how a well-known novelist, Agatha Christie, lives and "creates." By all accounts, Agatha was leading a life of a successful, personally fulfilled, happily married woman. But the next few years would prove to be telling ones for her.

Although her career had been moving steadily, her work was regarded as popular but "average." In 1926, Agatha Christie wrote her undisputed masterpiece which is still considered the classic novel in all detective fiction: *The Murder of Roger Ackroyd*. In a few short months, *Roger Ackroyd* would change Agatha Christie, the country matron who wrote as a pastime, into the leading mystery novelist in Britain—and in the world.

The Murder of Roger Ackroyd fits into the conventionally established rules of detective stories—or so it would seem. The story is once again set deep in Agatha Christie's own turf, the English countryside. Roger Ackroyd, a wealthy, well-liked gentleman, is found in his study, stabbed in the throat. There is the usual butler, who behaves suspiciously, and a coterie of other servants—a housekeeper, a parlormaid, two housemaids, a kitchenmaid, and a cook. There is the aid (or distraction) of various maps of the house and grounds.

Christie breaks one of her own rules about subduing characters to plot by creating a genuine comic character in the person of the narrator's sister, Caroline. The portrait of the good-natured but gossipy rumor-monger is painted with affectionate satire. The detective is once again Poirot, who dazzles characters and reader alike with his obscure questions that turn out to be devastatingly meaningful.

Although everything about *Roger Ackroyd* is highly entertaining, it was not this aspect that gained so much attention for its author. Agatha Christie now set her mark by breaking one of the rules of detective fiction: the thoughts of the "Watson" must not be concealed from the reader. Christie used a highly original trick of making the murderer the local doctor, the narrator of the story and, in this case, Poirot's "Watson." She had used a similar device in an earlier book, but it is safe to say that the ploy originated with her and had never been used by any other writer. Few if any readers caught on to the deceit before the end of the book. Fans of detective novels, and mystery writers themselves cried "Foul!" Dorothy Sayers, however, a brilliant contemporary of Christie's, called "Fair! and Fooled You!"

Agatha Christie would break many more rules in her career—from killing off every single character in the story (*Ten Little Indians*) to making every character the murderer (*Murder on the Orient Express*)—but *The Murder of Roger Ackroyd* was the first of her books to show her finest skills stretched to their fullest, most dazzling capacity.

The Murder of Rogert Ackroyd was published by Collins, who remain her British publishers to this day. John Lane & Company was bought by Dodd, Mead and Company; they became her American publishers.

Seven months after *The Murder of Roger Ackroyd* had brought her to the very pinnacle of fame, the world of Agatha Christie fell apart. She faced the first of two major upheavals in her life with little preparation. Mrs. Miller, her adored mother, died, leaving Agatha with an almost insurmountable grief. Agatha appeared to face her loss with the usual British stoicism. But it was not long after this that the chief constable of Surrey found himself faced with what he described as "the most baffling mystery ever set before me for solution." Agatha Christie had disappeared.

Agatha's green Morris automobile had been found abandoned on the South Downs not far from the Christie home. No note was found, nor was their any evidence of foul play. She was simply gone.

A force of 550 policemen, aided by bloodhounds, airplanes, tractors to break down the thickets, and 15,000 volunteers, took up the search. Descriptions of the 36-year-old authoress—height, 5 feet, 7 inches; gray eyes; reddish hair—were broadcast throughout the country. World-famous detectives and amateur sleuths, including Edgar Wallace, the popular mystery writer, and a former chief inspector of Scotland Yard, filled long newspaper columns with their ingenious speculations. Abduction, murder, and suicide were common guesses. But as the search dragged on, a nasty rumor spread that the clever inventor of mystery puzzles had cooked up her own disappearance as a publicity stunt. This news was promptly followed by howls of protest from British taxpayers, who demanded that the expensive womanhunt be called off.

Twelve days after her disappearance, the Yorkshire police received a call from the bandleader at a well-known resort hotel in Harrogate. He had noticed a resemblance between the circulated photograph of Agatha Christie and a hotel guest with a passion for music who joined members of the orchestra in singing and dancing. The following day the police verified that the guest, who was registered under the name of Mrs. Tessa Neele, was indeed the missing Mrs. Christie. The name she had taken in place of her own, Tessa Neele, was the identity of Colonel Archibald Christie's mistress.

It has since been established beyond question that Agatha was suffering from "classic" amnesia brought on by emotional strain and overwork. Faced with the loss of her mother and

the infidelity of Colonel Christie, she had suffered an emotional collapse. But at the same
time that she was caught in this terrible mental turmoil, she was subject to the most awful
press coverage and hounding. After she was
found, she suffered a complete nervous breakdown. Undoubtedly, her horror of publicity and
personal appearances dates back to those an-
guished days.

Much of the public believed that the entire
episode was a hoax to promote the already
best-selling *Murder of Roger Ackroyd*. Even today, some people insist that she was never registered at the spa in Yorkshire at all and that
she was actually hiding out in Cheshire near
Wilmslow at the home of a wealthy relative, a
Mr. Watts of the textile manufacturing company, S & J Watts. In view of the evidence,
however, the reality of Mrs. Christie's collapse
is patently obvious. The British press is known
for its merciless hounding of public figures and
it played a large part in Agatha Christie's
breakdown and subsequent attitude toward
publicity.

Agatha's marriage to Christie lasted fourteen years. The first six years of the marriage
were caught up in the excitement of the war.
The Christies were separated for long periods
and their brief encounters during those years
of world chaos were seen as romantic inter-

ludes. After the war, when they settled in Sunningdale, most of the excitement was Agatha's
as she gained increasing fame as a novelist.
The marriage settled into a kind of compla-
cency. Colonel Christie, accustomed to being
the flamboyant center of activity, looked for excitement elsewhere.

There were many who took it for granted
that Agatha Christie would never recover her
old brilliance after her collapse. They were
proved wrong almost immediately. Within a
year she was at work again, producing exactly
the same clear, highly methodical, brain-teas-
ing puzzles as before. *The Big Four* appeared
in 1927, followed by *The Mystery of the Blue
Train* in 1928. Both books showed off the tal-
ents of Hercule Poirot, not to mention the ingenious mind of their author.

"My husband found a younger woman,"
Agatha Christie would say many years later.
"Well, you don't write your own fate, your fate
comes to you." She divorced Christie in 1928.
He subsequently married the real Tessa Neele,
but Agatha retained her married name since
"Christie" was already well established among
readers of detective novels.

Chapter V

Fate Takes a Hand

Two years later, fate came to Agatha Christie in the person of Professor Max Mallowan, an eminent archeologist thirteen years younger than herself. Her second choice proved to be an entirely different type of man than Archibald Christie. Mrs. Christie still delights in quoting the lady who said, "It's wonderful to be married to an archeologist—the older you get the more interested he is in you." Agatha Christie married Max Mallowan on September 16, 1930, and they have been happily married for forty-five years, even though, she says, "he's so high-brow and I'm so lowbrow."

Professor Mallowan was professor of Western Asian archeology at London University at the time of their marriage. They met in Ur, honeymooned in Greece, and from that time on Agatha traveled with him wherever he went. They spent several years off and on in Nimrud, unearthing the story of murder, arson, and pillage which occurred in that Assyrian city in about 66 B.C. She helped clean the rare arrowheads, ivories, and pottery shards that were found. She photographed their finds painstakingly and, becoming impatient with the delay caused by sending her negatives back to England, was soon developing her own.

From this expedition and others like it, Professor Mallowan produced several classic works on archeology, including *25 Years of Mesopotamian Discovery* and *Excavation at Chagar Bazaar*. In 1966 he published the definitive work on excavations at the Biblical Callah: *Nimrud and Its Remains*. While the professor was about his business, his wife produced a few classic works of her own. *Murder in Mesopotamia* (1936), *Death on the Nile* (1937), *Appointment with Death* (1938), and *Death Comes as the End* (1945) all originate from her expeditions with her husband.

Of the four "expedition" books, Agatha Christie likes *Death on the Nile* best. "I think, myself," she says, "that the book is one of the best of my 'foreign travel' ones. I think the central situation is intriguing and has dramatic possibilities and the three characters, Simon, Linnet, and Jacqueline, seem to me to be real and alive." Certainly all four books are filled with color and adventure and give the reader the pleasure of seeing the world while he tries to solve the Christie puzzle.

One of Agatha Christie's most famous thrillers, *Murder on the Orient Express* (1934), derived from her travels with Professor Mallowan on the Orient Express to Baghdad. "On the way back," she says, "I was able to check on things I had thought about on the way out. I had to see where all the switches were. After he had read my book, one man actually made the journey to check up on this."

Throughout the 1930s and 1940s, Agatha Christie spun out tale after tale, producing a minimum of one detective novel a year and sometimes as many as four a year. She was as accomplished as she was prolific. She wrote four of her most widely acclaimed novels in a few brief years: *Lord Edgware Dies* (1933), *Murder on the Orient Express* (1934), *The ABC Murders* (1935), and *Ten Little Niggers* (1939).

The sheer number of her books would seem to indicate that they spring from her typewriter in whole form. But the facts are to the contrary. As much as she would like to give the impression that she doesn't give it much thought, Agatha Christie works deathly hard at writing. "You know how it is," she says, "an idea knocks about for months and you say, 'it would be rather interesting if one day I could manage that.'" When the writing day comes, she prefers it to be a wet one "because it's a shame to waste the weather."

In fact, a detective novel can take her anywhere from six weeks to three months to write. Once she has started, Christie writes quickly. By then her plot has been minutely outlined in her head. "The real work in my books is thinking out the developing of the story and worrying it until it comes right." She writes seated on a Chippendale chair at an oak table. She types on a portable typewriter (now electric) using three fingers of each hand. ("Most amateur typists can only use two," she says proudly.) Before she writes the first sentence, though, she roughs out the whole thing—complications, false trails, red herrings, the lot—down to the last detail. Then she begins with the last chapter first.

If there were any unfavorable effects from her earlier nervous collapse, they have never been manifested outwardly. Agatha Christie devotes herself to her work and to the work of her husband. At the same time, she prizes domestic life higher than literary success. She cooks with a passion and indulges in buying and redecorating houses. She also spends time playing the piano and collecting antique boxes, among other things. At the beginning of World

War II, Maurice Richardson, writing in *Picture Post*, noted: "In addition to her peculiar brand of ingenuity, Agatha Christie possesses that indispensable quality for any entertainer—charm. She is tall, rather broad, good-looking, smartly dressed, sophisticated without being affected, has a really sharp sense of humor. She is intelligent without being intellectual, takes a keen interest in food but doesn't drink or smoke, and loves music."

During World War II, Professor Mallowan joined the Royal Air Force and was loaned out to the British Military Government in North Africa. While he was there he became an adviser on Arab Affairs in Tripolitania. With her husband, albeit a different husband, once more caught up in the occupations of war, Agatha Christie also returned to wartime service, utilizing her World War I training to work in the dispensary of University College Hospital in London.

For a lady who claimed she didn't like writing ("It's so easy to be put off—any excuse rather than write"), Mrs. Christie seemed to do a lot of it. Not only did she continue to knock out several detective novels every year, but she also wrote under two pseudonyms. She had brought out a book of poems in 1925 called *The Road of Dreams*, which she published under her own name. After that, she decided that she would use pseudonyms when she wrote anything besides detective stories.

Altogether, she had written six romantic novels under the name of Mary Westmacott. The first, *Giant's Bread*, came out in 1930. She wrote three others before the secret of her identity was discovered by the *London Sunday Times* in 1949. *The Times* spilled the news that the writer of the romantically saccharine *The Rose and the Yew Tree* was none other than the Queen of Crime herself, Agatha Christie. One can fully appreciate the range of Mrs. Christie's technical skills when the mysteries are compared with the somewhat juvenile romantic novels. The novelist herself looks on the romantic novels as a hobby. "I found with straight novels that they didn't need much thinking out beforehand. Detective stories are much more trouble—even if you have no high ideals in writing them."

Her track record for completing a book involved one of these "straight novels," as she calls them. She wrote *Absent in the Spring* in one week in 1944. However, she said, she was quite exhausted at the end of it "and had to go to bed and rest."

It's possible that this was the only time Agatha Christie has rested in her entire life. Under her married name, Agatha Christie Mallowan, she wrote a witty travel book about archeology,

Come Tell Me How You Live, which appeared in 1946. And in 1965, under the same name, she produced *Star Over Bethlehem*, a sentimental collection of stories and poems with religious themes written for children. "They were rather fun to do," she says. "It's astonishing how one always wants to do something that isn't quite one's work. Like papering walls—which one does exceedingly badly, but enjoys because it doesn't count as work." Actually, Mrs. Christie probably papers walls rather well. In her lifetime she has completely redecorated no less than eighteen houses, doing much of the manual work herself.

As if all her wartime activity weren't enough, Agatha Christie began writing books at this time for posthumous publication. "I had plenty of time in the evenings; one didn't want to go out in the blitz," she explained. These works included her autobiography plus two full-length novels, said to be among her best. "One is Poirot's last case and one is, of course, Miss Marple's. I thought it a useful way of benefiting my relations; I gave one to my husband and one to my daughter—definitely made over to them, by deed of gift. So when I am no more they can bring them out and have a jaunt on the proceeds—I hope!"

Chapter VI

The Christie Cult

Over the years, an Agatha Christie cult has steadily grown. Agatha described some of the unique, if dubious, honors which have befallen her to Francis Wyndham: "I got one rather upsetting letter from a West African: 'I'm filled with enthusiasm for you and want you to be my mother. I'm arriving in England next month. . . .' I had to write back that I was going abroad indefinitely."

She also reported that "a terrible lot of girls" write fan letters from America. "They're always so earnest! And Indians are worse. 'I have loved all your books and think you must be a very noble woman.' Now what on earth is there in my books to make anybody think I'm *noble*? I'm afraid the fans are sometimes disappointed in my photographs—they write, 'I had no idea you were so old.' I get a good many asking curious questions: 'What emotions do you experience when you write?' All a *great* deal too sincere. What I'm writing is meant to be entertainment."

At a time in her life when one would expect work to taper off, Agatha Christie's career steams steadily ahead. Her fiftieth book, *A Murder Is Announced*, was published simultaneously nearly all over the world on June 5, 1960. Her British and American publishers issued a booklet filled with quotes from famous people, including the Prime Minister, praising the "Jubilee" of the Queen of Crime. Her publishers otherwise touted the event by spewing out press releases like confetti.

As in all major careers, the honors began to accrue. In January of 1956, Agatha Christie was elevated by Queen Elizabeth to the Order of the British Empire. She was also made a Fellow of the Royal Society of Literature and received an Honorary Doctorate of Letters from Exeter University. From that point on, it seemed that everyone expected Agatha Christie to slow down, if not indeed cease, production. In fact, she barely paused long enough to receive her award. Her grand total of titles soared to sixty books, then climbed dizzily up to seventy.

When Professor Mallowan was scheduled to lecture in Washington D.C. at the Freer Gallery in 1966, there was enormous public interest in whether or not Agatha Christie would accompany him. When the time came, there she was, right alongside him at all his interviews and sitting in the front row of the audience everywhere he spoke. The U.S. tour, sponsored by the Smithsonian Institute and the American Institute of Archeology, was an important milestone in the professor's career. His great work on Nimrud had just been published in America and, as one reporter noted, although his subjects had been dead a lot longer than any of his wife's corpus delicti, he gained a large and important audience.

A few years later, Agatha Christie celebrated her eightieth birthday with her eightieth book, *Passenger to Frankfurt*. The reviewer for *The New York Times Book Review* didn't like it very much, mostly because Mrs. Christie had departed from her customary environment and had embraced a plot that concerned "the current revolt of youth, the preoccupation with violence for its own sake, the pleasure seemingly derived from wholesale destruction." The reviewer seemed to think that Mrs. Christie had thrown herself admirably at these themes but had failed to realize them fully. The inference was that she should stick to what she knew best—a nice cozy murder in a country manor. But perhaps Agatha

Christie was approaching a time in her life when she had other things on her mind; certainly she was entitled to occupy herself with any theme she chose. Another *New York Times* columnist took the opposite tack, complimenting Mrs. Christie on her timeliness: "Last week, with attention still fixed on the airplane hijackings in the Middle East, Miss Christie came out with *Passenger to Frankfurt*, which just happens to include four hijackings." He also mentioned that even though she was admirably up-to-date, Agatha Christie wasn't too happy about modern sales methods and noted that she often sees her novels in supermarkets next to the baked beans. She lamented, "They'll soon be having these things at the butcher's."

Muriel Brown, reporting from London for *The Washington Post*, described Agatha Christie at this time as "a cheerful, bustling woman with a shock of white hair, a witty and lively mind, but with an intense shyness which makes it easier to picture her arranging flowers in church than as the world queen of crime stories. She has a positive dislike of television, plays the piano well, is a well-above-average cook, and she has been known to put money on horses."

Agatha Christie specializes in cooking "savory things" and believes that stoutness and happiness are forever united. She often has to skip the midday meal when she finds herself a little too "happy." She never drinks. "Though I have rolled it round and round my palate, I have never succeeded in liking it," she commented.

A year after *Passenger to Frankfurt* appeared, Queen Elizabeth once again selected the name of Agatha Christie for honors. She had previously received the O.B.E. and, as the wife of Sir Max Mallowan, she already was called Lady Mallowan. Now she was given the Order of Dame Commander of the British Empire. The problem of how she would keep her titles in line was solved when Agatha Christie said she would be Lady Mallowan when she was resting and Dame Agatha when she was working.

Yet another honor was bestowed on Dame Agatha in March of 1972 when she was approached by the management of Madame Tussaud's Wax Museum in London. They asked her to help with the creation of a figure of herself for their collection. The publicity-shy novelist happily submitted to measurements with tape measure and calipers. Dame Agatha, the Duchess of Death, was duly rendered in wax for the museum's Grand Hall by sculptor Lyn Kramer.

Age had not slowed Agatha Christie, but it seemed that fate would. While walking down a hallway at her Berkshire home, Winterbrook House, Dame Agatha fell and broke her hip. Ordinarly such an injury to a person in her eightieth year spells permanent invalidism. Despite this grim prognosis, Dame Agatha underwent surgery at Nuffield Orthopaedic Centre in Oxford and within months was back on her feet. That incident occurred over four years ago. She now gets about nicely, if somewhat gingerly, with only the help of a cane.

As if producing a book a year weren't enough, Dame Agatha dug up yet another project in 1972. She unearthed a play she wrote back in 1937. It is a kind of historical whodunnit that suggests that Akhnaton, the Egyptian Pharaoh who reigned from 1379 to 1362 B.C., was poisoned by his sister-in-law, Nezzmut. The name of the play is *Akhnaton*. Dame Agatha says she had forgotten all about the play until she found it when cleaning her house. Whether the play will ever be staged is speculative, given the enormous costs of staging. Unlike her more modern works, *Akhnaton* is a De Mille-sized production which requires a huge cast and lavish sets to define the period.

In 1974, at eighty-four years of age, Agatha Christie's greatest success still lay ahead of her. The most colorful and entertaining film of the year, perhaps even of the decade, was made from her mystery, *Murder on the Orient*

Express. Unlike many other films of her work, this one remained true to the original story and concept, filling the screen with nostalgia, humor, and intrigue. One of the most glamorous casts ever seen on film was assembled to do it, including Ingrid Bergman, Lauren Bacall, Richard Widmark, Anthony Perkins, Wendy Hiller, Rachel Roberts, and the enormously attractive Albert Finney as Hercule Poirot. Finney's perception of Poirot was as impeccable as the little detective himself, right down to his waved moustaches and the shiny black hair which he protected with a hairnet when he slept at night.

The entire whizbang production was directed with dashing style by Sidney Lumet, who allowed the actors to outrageously steal scenes from each other at every opportunity. If the movie was generally overacted, it was done with such enthusiasm, cleverness, and obvious mutual admiration among its stunningly professional cast that it heightened rather than distracted from the fascinating proceedings.

The great success of *Murder on the Orient Express* triggered what might well be the biggest coup in publishing. Apparently, the movie of *Orient Express* introduced a whole new generation of crime buffs to Agatha Christie and Hercule Poirot. The movie tie-in reissue of the book, brought out last year, has well over a million copies in print. But the biggest surprise was yet to come.

In March of 1975, after spirited competitive bidding among six paperback houses, the rights to Dame Agatha's new book, *Curtain*, went to Pocket Books for a guaranteed advance of $925,000! After the smoke cleared it was discovered that, since the hardcover version of the novel was not scheduled to appear until October of 1975, this might well be a record amount paid for a still unpublished book.

Curtain is one of the books Dame Agatha wrote at the peak of her powers in the 1940s. She originally intended it for posthumous publication. It is the swan song of Hercule Poirot. In view of the enormous public interest in the book, Dame Agatha apparently relented and agreed to allow the book to be published. The hoped for "jaunt" that she anticipated for her husband on the proceeds of the book she will now be able to enjoy right along with him. It could be a record-setting bash. From his share of the profits, Sir Max Mallowan could realize at least a million dollars.

Curtain, to bring Poirot full circle, is set at Styles, the country home that figured in his very first case, *The Mysterious Affair at Styles*. Despite the ballyhoo, the plot of *Curtain* is still a secret, but one way or another Poirot, "the nemesis of malefactors," is done in.

The Mallowans now divide their time between three beautiful homes—one in Chelsea, another at Wallingford on Thames in Berkshire, and a lovely square Georgian house, Greenway house, overlooking the river Dart in Devonshire, not far from Torquay. Of the three places, Agatha Christie feels she writes best in the Chelsea one: "In the country, there is always some nice distraction, and I'm only too eager for any excuse to stop work."

She remains as shy as ever, but even a lady as practiced as she in the art of avoiding publicity cannot help but reflect the glow of her recent accomplishments. "I always think it must end soon. Then I'm so glad when the next one comes along and it's not so difficult to think of something new after all. And, of course, as you get older you change, you see things from another angle. But probably I could write the same book again and again, and nobody would notice. Perhaps I'd better keep that up my sleeve, in case I ever run completely out of ideas."

What lies ahead for The Queen of Crime? Dame Agatha's philosophy can be found in one of her shorter works, a mystical tale called *The Man From The Sea*, in which life is described as "a gigantic drama under the order of a divine Producer," with no insignificant player or cue.

"I used it again," she says, "in *Towards Zero*, when a girl who has tried suicide is told that any moment before the end might be the important one. This I believe."

Chapter VII

Murder on the Stage

Agatha Christie has always claimed that she
enjoys writing plays more than books, finding
the technique more interesting, yet more difficult. Altogether she has written twelve plays,
five of them originals and seven adapted from
her own novels. Five more of her books have
been dramatized for the stage by other authors
and nine have been adapted for the screen.

Alibi, adapted by Michael Morton from *The
Murder of Roger Ackroyd*, was the first Agatha Christie to be dramatized. It opened in the
West End in 1928 and gave the young Charles
Laughton, in the role of Poirot, one of his first
leading parts in the London theater. *Alibi* left
Agatha Christie in near despair. The idea of
turning her little egg-headed Belgian into a
young lover thoroughly upset her. Her first

movie also was made from *Alibi*, with Austin Trevor starring as Poirot.

Agatha Christie tried her hand at a play writing in 1934 with *Black Coffee*, an original drama written directly for the stage. *Black Coffee* was generally well-received but then seemed to fade in the light of Mrs. Christie's later huge stage successes. Many years later, however, Howard Thompson, while reviewing another Christie revival for *The New York Times*, raised the spectre of the long-vanished play with a plaintive query: "Where, oh where, is her 1934 play ... *Black Coffee*?" There seems to be enough interest in the theatrical works of Mrs. Christie that it is likely that Mr. Thompson's plea will be answered sometime soon. A film version of *Black Coffee*, made in the 1940s, has likewise disappeared, but it may yet turn up on some late-night t.v. show.

In the late 1930s, two more of Mrs. Christie's works were adapted for the stage. In 1936 she collaborated with Frank Volper to stage her short story *Philomel Cottage*, which they called *Love from a Stranger*. *Love from a Stranger* was filmed twice. The first version starred Basil Rathbone and Ann Harding. A few years later John Hodiak and Sylvia Sidney played the leading roles in a second filming, which was titled *A Stranger Walked In*. A few years later her novel *Peril at End House* was adapted for the stage by Arnold Ridley, starring Francis L. Sullivan as Hercule Poirot.

The author was unhappy with all of these productions, yet she still felt that her work had potential for successful stage adaptation. She decided to adapt a play herself, choosing her book *Ten Little Niggers* as a vehicle. The drama opened at the St. James Theater in London in 1943 and played for 260 performances before it was bombed out by the blitz. Bombs aside, *Ten Little Niggers* has proved to be one of Agatha Christie's most enduring successes. It was produced in the United States a few years later and has been revived many times all over the world. Three separate screen versions have been filmed. The novelty of having every character bumped off fully captured the imagination of both the British and American public. Even though the plot is well known everywhere in the world today, its cleverness and originality is still thoroughly amusing.

There has always been a great deal of confusion and controversy over the play's title. *Ten Little Niggers* refers to a nursery rhyme. At the time the book was first published in 1939, the word "niggers" did not have the same connotation in England as it did in America. The title of Mrs. Christie's book demonstrates the isolationism and truly innocent bigotry that was common in the author's girlhood and is totally inappropriate now. England, one must remember, was a place where, less than twenty-five years ago, Winston Churchill could refer to Gandhi as "that little brown man in diapers." Agatha Christie based her title and plot on the original rhyme which was composed in America by Septimus Winner and later adapted in England by Frank Green in 1868. It goes as follows:

> Ten little nigger boys going out to dine,
> One choked his little self, and then there
>   were nine.
> Nine little nigger boys sat up very late,
> One overslept himself, and then there were
>   eight.
> Eight little nigger boys going down to De-
>   von,
> One got left behind, and then there were
>   seven.
> Seven little nigger boys chopping up
>   sticks,
> One chopped himself in half, and then
>   there were six.
> Six little nigger boys playing with a hive,
> A bumblebee stung one, and then there
>   were five.
> Five little nigger boys going in for law,
> One got in Chancery, and then there were
>   four.

Four little nigger boys sailing out to sea,
A red herring swallowed one, and then
 there were three.
Three little nigger boys going to the Zoo,
A big bear hugged one, and then there
 were two.
Two little nigger boys sitting in the sun,
One got frizzled up, and then there was
 one.
One little nigger boy left all alone,
He went and hanged himself, and then
 there were none.

When the Agatha Christie mystery was published in America it was felt necessary to
change the title. It was called *And Then There
Were None*; later it was called *Ten Little Indians*. The American audience then immediately
confused it with the following American
rhyme:

One little, two little, three little Indians,
Four little, five little, six little Indians,
Seven little, eight little, nine little Indians,
Ten little Indian boys. And there were:
Ten little, nine little, eight little Indians,
Seven little, six little, five little Indians,
Four little, three little, two little Indians,
One little Indian boy.

No one was ever quite sure after that, with the exception of Mrs. Christie herself, just which rhyme went with the title. To add further mix-up, the English rhyme originally ended with the sentence "He went and hanged himself, and then there were none." Mrs. Christie used this original ending in the novel. But she says that "He got married, and then there were none" was the popular ending in her childhood. When she adapted the book for the stage she decided, for dramatic reasons and also, one has to imagine, out of sheer perverse inventiveness, to change the plot around and use "He got married and then there were none" as the ending. That's why so many people insist that so many other people don't know what they're talking about when they tell the story of *Ten Little Niggers*. As G.C. Ramsey says, "If you have only seen one of the stage or screen versions, you will be even more amazed at the ingenuity of the original ending" as demonstrated in the novel.

Ten Little Niggers was made for the movies on three separate occasions. The first, in 1945, starred Barry Fitzgerald and Walter Huston and was released in the United States with the title *And Then There Were None*. The second version, starring Wilfred Hyde-White, Stanley Holloway, and an assorted international cast, was made in 1965 and was called *Ten Little In-*

dians. An even more recent film was made in 1974.

The novel itself had no less than three American titles. The first, appearing in March 1940, was *And Then There Were None.* Subsequent editions called it *Ten Little Indians* and *The Nursery Rhyme Murders.*

One would think that enough commotion had been caused over the mystery's name, but in October of 1966 another flap arose when the play was revived in Birmingham, England, under its original title. More than twenty members of the Coordinating Committee Against Racial Discrimination paraded in front of the theater as customers waited in line to purchase tickets. One placard-carrying demonstrator carried a sign giving the *Oxford Dictionary* definition of the word *nigger*—"a contemptuous reference to colored people." The committee's chairman pointed out that the title had been changed for the United States and demanded the same for England. Without argument, the producers quietly complied with the request.

The final years of World War II saw no more Agatha Christies in the West End. But as soon as the lights were on again, she adapted her 1937 "expedition" mystery, *Death on the Nile,* for the stage, retitling it *Murder on the Nile.* (She also had written a short story called *Death on the Nile,* but the story had no relation to either the novel or to the subsequent stage play.)

Agatha Christie rested from her theatrical pursuits for the next few years, preferring to devote herself to travel, novels, and archeology. But in the 1950s she was once more on the boards; from that time on there seems to have been at least one Christie play on the London stage every year. *Murder at the Vicarage*, the original Miss Marple book, was adapted by Moie Charles and Barbara Toy in 1950. *The Hollow*, from the novel of the same name, was adapted by Agatha Christie herself in 1951.

Agatha Christie learned a great deal about theater from these early efforts. In fact, she was to demonstrate as much theatrical savvy in the future as she had previously displayed knowledge of poisons and puzzles. In the following two years she wrote two of the greatest successes ever produced in English-speaking theater: *The Mousetrap* and *Witness for the Prosecution*.

When the late Queen Mary asked for an original Agatha Christie play as part of a BBC radio program commemorating her eightieth birthday, she started something that the British drama critics have never quite forgiven. Agatha Christie wrote *Three Blind Mice* for Her Majesty, then subsequently adapted the radio script into a short story and later a play. The play, entitled *The Mousetrap*, has been playing continuously eight times a week on the London stage ever since. Now reeling into its twenty-fourth year, it is the longest-running play in world theater history, having zeroed in on and passed up that age-old antique *The Drunkard* (which purportedly ran for twenty-two years, although no one can quite remember the exact figure).

The Mousetrap has been translated into 22 languages; it was presented in 41 countries; it employed more than 180 actors and actresses in its eight roles; and it has taken in close to $8 million at the box office.

The setting is Monkswell Manor, a large, drafty old house which the heroine has inherited from an aunt. She and her husband decide to turn it into a guest house. The mischief starts when a detective sergeant and five disparate guests, who have nothing in common but the blizzard that drove them inside for shelter, join the couple. Somehow it is explained how Monkswell Manor is linked to a recent London murder.

The Mousetrap opened on November 25, 1952. *The London Sunday Times* said of that first night: "There is none of this hiding of vital facts in Mrs. Christie. She keeps the audience moving step by step with her detective. It is this honesty of procedure that puts Mrs.

Christie so high in ranks of police novel writing." Stanley Sparks, writing for *The Morning Advertiser*, said, "Agatha Christie is like a perfect hostess serving hemlock at a cocktail party." And a critic with *Weekly Sporting Review* wrote, "We have all of us been well and truly diddled."

Dame Agatha once commented, "When I wrote it [*The Mousetrap*], I rather thought I'd fallen between the two schools of comedy and thriller. I thought it was a nice little play that might run a year or eighteen months." She accommodatingly deeded the royalties over to her grandson Mathew Prichard. He was then twelve years old. Mathew is now thirty-five and a very wealthy gentleman farmer in Wales. He has three children, the eldest of whom is named Alexandra Agatha. Mathew's grandmother says she "worries he may never need to look for a job."

The endless run of *The Mousetrap* has been marked by several anniversaries. The first celebration was in the fifth year of its run, when the play tallied 2,239 performances, outstripping by one performance the previous British record-holder, *Chu-Cin-Chow*, which had closed in 1922. In five years, nearly a million people had seen *Mousetrap*. The producer, Peter Saunders, tossed a glittering soiree at the Savoy Hotel to tout the occasion. Rumor was that the shy Mrs. Christie might not appear at her own party. But she turned up at the banquet without a ticket and was stopped at the door. "I know many people don't know me," she said. "But authors are shy people—we prefer to stay at home. But they did let me in."

The party was London's biggest theatrical bash in years. The guests, who included Richard Attenborough, Ian Carmichael, Margaret Lockwood, Julie Andrews, Anna Neagle and a hundred other dazzling names, demolished more than 700 bottles of champagne. One well-known, youngish actor said, "If Mrs. Christie offered me a part in a new play I wouldn't accept—I wouldn't live as long as it would run." Five actresses who had played the leading lady role during the play's run were also there: Sheila Sim, Joan Harvey, Marguerite Stone, Heather Stannard, and Mary Law. Little did they know that their number would increase by nineteen over the next fifteen years.

John Mills presented Mrs. Christie with a gold replica of the theater program which marked the record-setting run. She in turn presented Richard Attenborough, who starred in the play when it first opened, with a gold mousetrap for the Ambassador Theater.

During the speeches which followed the presentation, playwright Sir Alan Herbert

posed the question: "How has this gentle crea-
ture been obsessed for forty-eight years with
vile murder? She discovered that all men love
puzzles and that nearly all women have a great
inclination towards homicide."

At the party's end, Mrs. Christie nervously
faced a battery of press photographers and television cameramen. "I am not good at
speeches," she said. "I'd rather write ten plays
than make one speech."

The five-year party was only the beginning.
In 1962, the male lead at curtain call shouted
into the audience, "We're going into our tenth
year. If you tell your friends who did it we
may have to close in a couple of years." One
lady, seeing *Mousetrap* for the first time, said,
"Ten years and nobody's told me who did the
killing. That wouldn't be sporting, now would
it? English people are loyal. If they tell you not
to tell, you don't tell."

Either the plot of *The Mousetrap* was indeed
the best-kept secret in town, or there was something else behind its phenomenal success, because on November 25, 1973, Peter Saunders
launched yet another anniversary party at the
Savoy. This time 600 actors, actresses, and others connected with the production throughout
its history were present, including twenty-one
of the twenty-four leading ladies. Once more
Sheila Sim and her husband, Richard Attenbo-

rough, the two original leads of the show, toasted the Queen of Crime, Dame Agatha Christie.

Asked for his explanation of the success of his grandmother's play, Mathew Prichard said, "It is good, clean, family entertainment. I look forward to the day when I take my three children to see it." The playwright herself said, "I think really it is probably because it is the sort of play you can take anyone to. It is not really frightening. It is not really horrible. It is not really a farce. But it has got a little bit of all those things. After about the eighteenth time I decided it was well-constructed. The interest keeps up and that's difficult."

It's true that the interest does keep up, but the lines and exposition are old-fashioned beyond belief. ("By the time the snow has melted a *lot* of things may have happened".) Nevertheless, the play charges happily along on the London stage, sending out dozens of additional companies all over the world. The Arena Stage presented it at the Hippodrome in the United States in 1955, and it is currently playing at the National Arts Theater off Broadway in New York.

Apart from the nearly annual change of cast, the passage of the years has incorporated some updatings. There are no longer references to rationing and identity cards. In 1970 an "absconding bank clerk" turned into a "drug pusher," and inflation has been recognized. In 1952 the weekly charge at the guest house was 18 dollars. It is currently around 50 dollars.

Not surprisingly, there have been many criticisms of the play and some complaints. "By cornering the Ambassador for so many years," wrote Nicholas De Jongh, a reporter for *The Guardian Arts*, "Mr. Peter Saunders must have deprived other theater managers of the opportunity of presenting daring, experimental, or difficult plays." Perhaps taking note of the criticism, on March 24, 1974, after 8,860 performances, *The Mousetrap* changed theaters, moving from the Ambassador to the St. Martin, where it is still going strong.

Unquestionably, *The Mousetrap* is a museum piece. Along with the Changing of the Guard and London Tower, it has become a tourist attraction. No one seems to know quite why, except that to see it recalls, like the Tower and the Guards, an England that was strong in the past—strong enough to remain glimmering in the present, although it vanished some time ago.

Witness for the Prosecution, originally a short story, opened to stunning reviews in London in November of 1953. A year later it was welcomed with great pleasure in New York, receiving the New York Drama Arts' Circle

Award. In a leading role, Francis L. Sullivan, the Poirot of *Peril at End House*, garnered lavish praise from Brooks Atkinson: "He is Sir Wilfred, the defense counselor. He gives a grandiloquent performance with an undertone of humor. Imperiously realistic on the surface, he has his tongue in his cheek. By the breadth of his playing he represents the true spirit of the murder mystery. It's a game. In the twists of the plot and the expertness of the playing, *Witness for the Prosecution* is one of the best."

Critics and audiences in both England and America were thrilled by the play's quirky, startling, triple-twist climax. W.A. Darlington wrote of the London production, "You can never trust her [Mrs. Christie] to have finished till the curtain is irrevocably down. Naturally, I am not going to spoil her story for you by giving away the superb double twist by which she brings down the curtain. All that can fairly be said here is that the final scene shows at its best this writer's gift for making the explanation you had never thought of seem quite obvious once you've been told. Success, then, stares Agatha Christie in the eye."

This grand reception from the press was more than just another feather in Dame Agatha's hat. Before the play opened, the producers had asked her to change the ending, leaving out the final twist, which they found too ingenious. Mrs. Christie refused flatly. She had been perfectly agreeable about all other changes in her script, cutting dialogue and writing new lines wherever it was required. But she would not budge an inch on the ending. "Oh, she didn't argue," said Patricia Jessel, who created the title role of "the witness" both in London and America, "she only said this was how she had always intended the scene to be, and she believed it was right. Nearly everybody else, though, felt a little shaky about it."

Dame Agatha's judgment was unerring. The play was a tremendous hit and audiences and critics alike were cautioned not to reveal the "twist" ending. Audiences were so enamored of the surprise curtain that they readily complied with the management's request. Soon everyone was talking about the bizarre ending of Mrs. Christie's new play, but no one, unless he had actually seen it, knew what it was.

Mrs. Christie got such a boot out of the whole thing that she said, "I must say, I did enjoy the first night of that play. Usually it's hideous. I always feel very shy and uncomfortable appearing in public, but that was heaven. The play was so well done, and there were quantities of women waiting for me outside the theater—quite rough types you know; but they really welcomed me, patted me on the back and said 'Well done, dearie!' "

The film rights to *Witness for the Prosecution* were sold for 116,000 pounds. It is Agatha Christie's favorite movie. Charles Laughton, the original Poirot of *Alibi*, played Sir Silfred; Elsa Lanchester ministered unto his crotchety demands. Marlene Dietrich was "the witness," and Tyrone Power was marvelous as the ingratiating Leonard Vole.

Riding high on the crest of these two enormous successes, Mrs. Christie followed them right up with an original drama called *Spider's Web* which ran a total of 577 performances, over 100 performances more than *Witness* ran. *Spider's Web* is a highly polished example of Christie stagewriting set in the usual drawing room of a Kent manor house. The film version starred Glynis Johns and John Justin. In 1974 *The Spider's Web* enjoyed a revival at Lolly's Theater Club in New York. Howard Thompson of *The New York Times* described it thus: "Dame Agatha's nimble, ironic teasing and the cast's personable acting . . . clearly held the packed family audience, with children leaning forward, too. Christie readers exchanged murmurs, 'Well—who did it?' "

In 1956 Mrs. Christie collaborated with Gerald Verner to adapt her novel *Towards Zero* for the stage. This was followed by two other original plays, *The Unexpected Guest* and *Verdict*, both appearing in 1958. *The Unexpected*

Guest was another Christie rule-breaker, since the audience knows from the beginning who committed the murder—the curtain rises on a dead man in a wheelchair and his wife with revolver in hand, as a stranded motorist bursts in on the scene.

About this time Mrs. Christie seemed to lose some of her interest in playwriting. She wrote only two more plays in the 1960s, *Go Back for Murder* (1960), based on her novel *Five Little Pigs*, and *Rule of Three*, three original one-act plays which were produced in 1962. But although she is no longer active in the theater, her plays seem to have a momentum of their own. Currently in New York are new Agatha Christie revivals: *The Mousetrap* and *The Spider's Web*. Also touring the U.S. is the American musicalized version of *Ten Little Indians*, called *Somethings Afoot*. The authors of the musical claim that their version is a compilation of several Christie stories but admit that the action takes place on an island where all ten characters meet their end.

Several additional movies have been made from Christie thrillers. Austin Trevor played Hercule Poirot in the film version of *Lord Edgware Dies* and Tony Randall took over that role in *The Alphabet Murders*, which was derived from *The ABC Murders*.

Margaret Rutherford joyously created Miss

Marple for several "Murder" films, including *Murder at the Gallop*, *Murder Most Foul*, and *Murder She Said*.

Dame Agatha is not nearly as enthusiastic about movies as she is about the stage. "I kept off films for years," she says, "because I thought they'd give me too many heartaches. Then I sold the rights to MGM, hoping they'd use them for television. But they chose films. It was too awful! They did things like taking a Poirot and putting Miss Marple in it! And all the climaxes were so poor, you could see them coming! I get an unregenerate pleasure when I think they're not being a success. They wrote their own script for the last one—nothing to do with me at all—*Murder Ahoy*. One of the silliest things you ever saw. It got a very bad review, I'm delighted to say."

Dame Agatha's dissatisfaction has been so great that it is unlikely that many more films will be made from her works. But she's a lady who wreaks success wherever she goes, so one can imagine that she may be filming and directing her own films any time now.

Chapter VIII

Mrs. Christie's Detectives

A prominent businessman once said: "The best you can do is try to buy low, sell high, save your money, and hope for a decent obituary in the *New York Times*."

The front page of the *Times* is reserved for those stories of the greatest national importance. Practically no story gets any more plan than a two or, at best, a three column headline. On Wednesday, August 6, 1975, there were no three column headlines, no story was important enough. The stories that rated two columns were: "Terrorists in Malaysia Release 9," "Change in City Charter Proposed to Curb Mayor's Powers," "Investigators in Hoffa Case looking for Foster Son," and "Hercule Poirot Is Dead; Famed Belgian Detective."

If nothing else could, this final word on Hercule Poirot secures his place as one of the greatest of the world's detectives. Here are some excerpts from the *Times* obituary of the man who many millions will mourn. The byline belonged to John Lask.

"Hercule Poirot, a Belgian detective who became internationally famous, has died in England. His age was unknown.

"Mr. Poirot achieved fame as a private investigator after he retired as a member of the Belgian police force in 1904. His career, as chronicled in the novels of Dame Agatha Christie, his creator, was one of the most illustrious in fiction.

"At the end of his life, he was arthritic and had a bad heart. He was in a wheelchair often, and was carried from his bedroom to the public lounge at Styles Court, a nursing home in Essex, wearing a wig and false mustaches to mask the signs of age that offended his vanity. In his active days, he was always impeccably dressed.

"The news of his death, given by Dame Agatha, was not unexpected. Word that he was near death reached here last May.

"Dame Agatha reports in 'Curtain' that he managed, in one final gesture, to perform one more act of cerebration that saved an innocent bystander from disaster. 'Nothing in his life became him like the leaving it,' to quote Shakespeare, whom Poirot frequently misquoted."

M. Hercule Poirot

A nondescript crowd of Belgian refugees excited her curiosity. What, she wondered, were they like at home—these sad, uprooted people? What had they done before the guns of August 1914 boomed and the Germans swiftly and savagely raped their land? Were they men of substance perhaps: bankers, bakers, doctors, butchers? One, maybe, was a murderer; one could have been a detective. She decided one might be a detective. From her imagination was born the neat little man with egg-shaped head, a passion for neatness, and a fervid reliance on his "little grey cells."

The story may be apocryphal, but Hercule Poirot was born, at an age when he had long since retired from active duty, at the end of World War I. He was born with a past. Little bits and pieces of that past have been given to us by Mrs. Christie over the years, but on our first meeting with Poirot we get only the bare essentials.

The introduction to Hercule Poirot is provided by his first biographer—his "Watson"— Captain Hastings, about whom Mrs. Christie has said: "I got very tired of Captain Hastings. . . . Quite early on I banished him to the Argentine. But I think he came back once. . . ." Hastings tells us that Poirot is a

Belgian refugee, one of those who escaped the German onslaught. He had been, in his time, one of the most accomplished and celebrated detectives of the Belgian police. He had unraveled many baffling mysteries with an ability for detection that was truly extraordinary. This physical description in *The Mysterious Affair at Styles*, is brief, but now famous:

"Poirot was an extraordinary-looking little man. He was hardly more than five feet, four inches, but carried himself with great dignity. His head was exactly the shape of an egg, and he always perched it a little on one side. His moustache was very stiff and military. The neatness of his attire was almost incredible. I believe a speck of dust would have caused him more pain than a bullet wound."

Hercule Poirot is clearly not a dashing lover. You will not find him dallying in some villianess' arms . . . or bed. He is not hard-boiled, devil-may-care, handsome, or irresistible. Poirot does not pummel criminals into an insensible, quivering, penitent jelly. Nor do they lay a hand on him. He does not carry a Beretta, or a snub-nosed thirty-eight. But Hercule Poirot is one of only three or four fictional detectives who have achieved an almost lifelike quality and practically historical significance. The four have a great deal in common. They are all physically unprepossessing, sometimes even grotesque, and intensely cerebral. They are all eccentric to the point of being very odd. And they all have monstrous egos. They are Sherlock Holmes, Hercule Poirot, Lord Peter Wimsey, and Nero Wolfe. They are the most famous detectives of all time.

For enormously popular heroes, they are unusual, to say the least. Each is perhaps best known by his weaknesses and vices, traits they share in full measure. Sherlock Holmes, the father of them all, is a terrible showoff and a drug addict to boot. Poirot is dandified and dyes his hair. Lord Peter is often silly and wears a monocle. Nero Wolfe is petulant, terrified of the least amount of physical exertion, and he eats.

Only one of these heroes, Lord Peter, has had any love life to speak of. And Wimsey's wooing of Harriet Vane is more a meeting of the minds and a battle of wills than a romance.

We know little of them as whole people. They are, by and large, not much more than two-dimensional. The great Holmes, in fact, has one interest only. His widely varied and multifaceted knowledge is singlemindedly focused on crime. When Watson expresses surprise over Holmes' lack of knowledge about the Earth and its place in the universe, Holmes replies that now that he knows, he will do his best to forget it. "The mind, my dear Watson, is like an attic. Only so much furniture will fit. That which does not add to my ability to solve a crime is excess, and must be discarded."

These men are decidedly lacking in the standards of virtues we usually set for our literary heroes. And yet, they are pre-eminently the favorites of millions. While there are many similarities among them, they are also quite different.

The first words ever spoken by Holmes, Wimsey, and Poirot are interesting. They give an indication of character at a time when each is not self-conscious about his coming fame and notoriety.

Holmes is, as he will always be, correct and boastful.

Lord Peter's introduction is self-deprecating and flippant, which is at once a large part of his character and his disguise.

Hercule Poirot is at once effusive and ingratiating.

They are different and they are the same, these giants of detective fiction. In character, method, in personality they differ. Where they are the same is in a brilliant devotion to the brilliant solution of brilliant puzzles.

What we know about Poirot is spotty. It is,

after all, the puzzle that dominates an Agatha Christie mystery. But Dame Agatha tells us about Poirot, little by little. And by this time, there is surely enough for a detailed biography of the little Belgian.

Since he came upon us, not in the full bloom of his youth, but in his declining years as a semiretired detective, we must conjecture about his past with the facts that Agatha Christie has given us.

His age, for example, at this writing is somewhere around 126 years. It is possible that he is quite a few years younger, since that figure is calculated on a retirement date of 1904, revealed to us in the first Poirot—*The Mysterious Affair at Styles*. That is often taken to mean that he was sixty-five in 1904 and would today be 136. But he could have retired after thirty years on the Belgian police at say, fifty. He would then be 121 today. He could even be younger, but since he ceased to age around fifty years ago, the point is moot. It is sufficient to say that Hercule Poirot has had a good long run.

He is no old fogey. In furniture, he prefers the geometric lines of comfortable modern. What he most prefers to sit on we would call Art Deco today—a style in the midst of a popular renaissance.

Poirot enjoys good food and wines. He has

put away some Chateau Monton Rothschild, an impeccable first-growth Bordeaux (called claret in England), which sells for astronomical sums in the U.S. He is not addicted to English tea and prefers instead his morning coffee and afternoon chocolate.

Poirot does not tend toward the traditional English flower gardening, but is taken with the cultivation of vegetable marrows. (For quite a long time many Americans have been puzzled by Poirot's vegetable marrows. "Those great swollen green things that taste of water?" says Dr. Burton, a friend of Poirot. I myself have envisoned something like Triffids, seething and boiling, with their roots in the bog. Vegetable marrow is, however, no more than the British word for squash, or zucchini.) According to Poirot, the flavor of the marrow can be improved by cultivation. "It can be given," he says, "a bouquet."

There is a dark spot in Poirot's past, as we discover in the *Labors of Hercules*:

"—You also had a brother called Achille, did you not?" Poirot's mind raced back over the details of Achille Poirot's career. Had all that really happened?

"Only for a short space of time," he replied.

We have never met a Mme. Poirot or Poirot *fils* or *filles*, but M. Poirot, unlike many of his fellow bachelor detectives, is no misogynist. He likes women and is incurably romantic. As part of the denoument in many a case, M. Poirot unites the young lovers or saves a faltering marriage. And he does not eschew some glimmer of romance from his own past, either as we learn in the *Labors of Hercules*:

"It is the misfortune of small, precise men to hanker after large and flamboyant women. Poirot had never been able to rid himself of the fatal fascination the Countess held for him."

Countess Vera Rossakoff is a figure from Poirot's dim past. Poirot is struck with admiration for the way she steals jewels, for her faded beauty and aristocratic ways. She is a woman in a thousand, maybe in a million!

Poirot's secretary, the efficient Miss Lemon, asks if it is all right to pay an enormous florist's bill for red roses to the Countess. Poirot replies. (Also from the *Labors of Hercules*):

"There are moments," he said, "when

one does not economize." Humming a little tune he went out the door. His step was light ... Miss Lemon stared after him ... all her feminine instincts were aroused.

"Good gracious ... I wonder ... Really at his age! ... Surely not. ..."

Hercule Poirot has become more and more anachronistic with time. It is just that, according to Mrs. Christie, "a private detective who takes cases just doesn't exist these days, so it becomes more difficult to involve him and make him convincing in so doing." And in the long run, Mrs. Christie has run out of affection for Hercule Poirot. "He bores me to death," said Dame Agatha. But for the fact that he is such a moneymaker, she would have poisoned him long ago. "I can't kill him," she continues, "because if I did I'd only have to invent stories of what he did before he died, which is more difficult. However, I can put him in a wheelchair."

Mrs. Christie did, however, eventually decide to do the old gentleman in. While we may not know the date of his birth, we now know the date of the death of Hercule Poirot. It is October, 1975, when the latest and last Poirot novel will be published. The last adventure is in *Cur-*

tain, originally written by Agatha Christie during the London blitz in 1944.

There may be no more new Poirot chronicles, but Agatha Christie has made sure that the little Belgian's place in history is secure. There are innumerable adventures and novels for the future fan to discover. Three generations of readers have already matched wits with Hercule Poirot. There will be many more.

Miss Jane Marple

If, as it has been said, Hercule Poirot is a cartoon Frenchman (albeit in Belgian clothing), then Miss Jane Marple is certainly a cartoon Englishwoman. Like Poirot, she has not aged in almost fifty years. She too was born elderly.

Miss Marple has been likened to Agatha Christie herself, but Dame Agatha rejects the comparison. "I don't have Jane Marple's guilty-till-proven-innocent attitude," she says. "But, like Jane, I don't accept surface appearances." While Mrs. Christie thinks Poirot has become unreal, she feels the problem does not arise with Miss Marple. "There are still plenty of them drifting about," she says.

Miss Jane Marple is a tall, thin, elderly lady with china-blue eyes and a wrinkled face. She is all pink and white and fluffy and is always in the midst of some knitting which is also fluffy.

Agatha Christie first introduces us to Miss Marple in her 1930 novel, *Murder at the Vicarage*:

> "Miss Marple is a white-haired old lady with a gentle, appealing manner—Miss Wetherly is a mixture of vinegar and gush. Of the two, Miss Marple is much the more dangerous."

She is one of a type, those elderly English ladies living in a genteel but simple manner on a fixed income which buys less every year. She is not a lady of the town, having her hair done once a week, afternoon tea in the little shop that carries the wonderful scones, two matinees a month in the cheapest seats. She is country English. Gardening and long walks and stout, serviceable shoes. She lives in the hamlet of St. Mary Mead and receives some financial aid from her nephew in town, novelist Raymond West, who does not think much of life in the country.

> "I regard St. Mary Mead," he said authoritatively, "as a stagnant pool."

"That is really not a very good simile, dear Raymond," said Miss Marple briskly. "Nothing, I believe, is so full of life under the microscope as a drop of water from a stagnant pool."

Miss Marple feels, rather simply, that human nature is quite the same everywhere, but it is more difficult to observe in a city. It certainly seems as though human nature is as inclined to murder as much in St. Mary Mead as anywhere.

Both of Mrs. Christie's major characters walk about with a bit of shock value. When Hercule Poirot arrives in an English country house, complete with accent and patent leather shoes, his presence is as out of place as the body on the floor of the library. Miss Marple, on the other hand, blends into the landscape so well that the realization that this genteel, elderly lady is discussing murder knowledgeably and with aplomb also causes shock.

Miss Marple solves her murders using the same tools as Hercule Poirot—logic, psychology, and an intimate knowledge of human nature. It is not necessary for her to have traveled around the world to solve the mysteries of the worldly. Has a reknowned physician been murdered? It reminds Miss Marple of the grocery clerk who was poisoned. The disappearance of a ring belonging to an American starlet seems to Miss Marple just like the time that Mrs. Twickenham's cat was missing for a week. There *are* psychological parallels. By following them in each case and using common sense and knowledge of human nature, Miss Marple solves the mystery.

Many actors, from Francis Sullivan and Charles Laughton to the brilliant Albert Finney, have portrayed Hercule Poirot, but the role of Jane Marple belongs totally to Margaret Rutherford. Although she was a little heavier and more active than the fictional Jane Marple, Miss Rutherford, acting in the series of Miss Marple films, came to be the symbol of all the Miss Marples in England.

Before the actress' death last year, Mrs. Christie, who was two years older than Miss Rutherford, was asked about Miss Rutherford's portrayals of Jane Marple.

"Very nice," she said. "I know her, yes, but not very well. To me, she's always looked like a bloodhound." This comment is perhaps not surprising when one recalls that Mrs. Christie has been frankly critical of the movies' treatment of her books in general.

Mrs. Christie has a soft spot for Miss Marple and prefers her amateur's dash to Poirot's professional hauteur. And she has

aged Miss Marple ever so slightly. Since she
was described as old forty-five years ago, you
might expect Miss Marple to be at least in a
rocking chair. But no, she still manages to get
about a good deal, although she can't garden as
much as she used to. Jane Marple also keeps
abreast of the times.

Although she may not talk about it, Jane
Marple seems to know a little bit about everything and a great deal about what you *really*
mean when you tell her something. One young
woman was discussing the plan of a murder
she secretly intended to commit. She described
a hypothetical case that had taken place sometime in the past, but Jane Marple quickly dis-
couraged her.

"... give up the idea ... I beg of you,"
said Miss Marple.

"I think I shall," the girl mused. "There
might be other Miss Marples."

Tommy and Tuppence Beresford

"Tommy, old thing!"
"Tuppence, old bean!"

Thus do two friends meet in 1922, solve a mystery, and pledge their troth in the first Tommy and Tuppence book, *The Secret Adversary*. The adjective "old" is just a British endearment and should not be taken literally. Here are two Agatha Christie detectives who are not in their dotage. According to Mrs. Christie, their combined ages would "not have totalled forty-five."

At the time of their reunion, Lieutenant Thomas Beresford (Tommy), and Miss Prudence Cowley (Tuppence), have just been "demobbed" (demobilized) from service in the Great War. At loose ends and looking for adventure, they stumble over a mystery to keep them occupied.

Tuppence has been a nurse and Tommy has been an officer in intelligence work—twice wounded. The excitement and danger of wartime work has made them restless with peacetime activity.

Tuppence is a character in a situation with which we can readily identify Mrs. Christie. At the end of the war, Agatha Christie had just begun to write her mysteries. She was a demobilized nurse and her husband, Archibald Christie, had been a daring flying officer. It was well-known that Christie sorely missed the excitement and danger of the war. The dedication of *The Secret Adversary* is:

"To all those who lead monotonous lives in the hope that they may experience at second hand the delights and dangers of adventure."

By 1929, when the second Tommy and Tuppence book, *Partners in Crime*, appears, the Christie marriage had been dissolved, but Tommy and Tuppence had married. The birth of twins put an end to their detective adventures—for the time being.

In 1941, we meet the Beresfords again in *N or M?* Mrs. Christie does not slow time for them, as she does for Poirot and Miss Marple. Rather, she accelerates it, since their son Derek, who would be twelve years old, is a lieutenant in the R.A.F.

The Beresfords have mellowed over the years and we can easily conjure an image of the Mallowans, contented in their later life, from Tommy and Tuppence in *Postern of Fate* (1973). They are comfortable, but still intrigued by life; relaxed, but not willing to just watch the parade pass by.

Mrs. Ariadne Oliver

In February 1966, Francis Wyndham wrote about an exclusive interview he'd gained with Agatha Christie in *The London Times*: "The popular image of her as a Miss Marple, twittering but beady, is false; there's nothing spinsterish about her and she seems more middle-aged than old. If she appears in her books at all, it's as Mrs. Ariadne Oliver, the comfortably cultured matron who occasionally plays second string to Poirot."

Mrs. Oliver pops up quite often in Agatha Christie's books, usually as a foil for Poirot. She is a lady mystery writer who caricatures those of that ilk. While Mrs. Christie has surely given us some of her own characteristics in Mrs. Oliver, the fictional detective writer just doesn't measure up to Mrs. Christie in her work.

Mrs. Oliver's tales are usually highly implausible and when she investigates a "real" murder with Poirot, she often takes advantage of hindsight to change the name of the person she suspected.

Certainly Dame Agatha pokes some wry fun at both the genre and herself through Mrs. Oliver. Quite often the source of the joke is Mrs. Christie's well-known penchant for decorating houses as we discover in the *Third Girl*:

"These cherries—they are new?" He waved a teaspoon. It was, he felt, rather like being in a cherry orchard.

"Are there too many of them, do you think?" said Mrs. Oliver. "So hard to tell beforehand with wallpaper. Do you think my old one was better?"

Poirot cast his mind back dimly to what he seemed to remember as large quantities of bright-colored tropical birds in a forest. He felt inclined to remark *"Plus ça change, plus c'est la même chose"* but restrained himself.

Superintendent Battle

While Agatha Christie has most often used the police in the classic detective-novel way—as a bumbling foil for the detective—she has written about a policeman who appears occasionally in her books without his foot in his mouth.

Superintendent Battle of the C.I.D. will sometimes solve a case all by himself. While he has not the same sort of personality as the policeman created by Ngaio Marsh, Superintendent Roderick (Handsome) Alleyn, Battle can hold his own with the likes of Inspectors French and Japp as we discover in *The Secret of Chimneys*:

"You're a cheerful fellow, Battle. When will you get me, I wonder?"

"Plenty of rope, sir," quoted the superintendent, "plenty of rope."

"In the meantime," said Anthony, "I am still the amateur assistant?"

"That's it, Mr. Cade."

"Watson to your Sherlock, in fact?"

"Detective stories are mostly bunkum," said Battle unemotionally. "But they amuse people," he added, as an afterthought. "And they're useful sometimes."

"In what way?" asked Anthony curiously.

"They encourage the universal idea that the police are stupid. When we get an amateur crime, such as a murder, that's very useful indeed."

Mr. Parker Pyne

"Are you happy? If not, consult Mr. Parker Pyne, 17 Richmond Street." The above advertisement was run daily on the front page of the *Times* just often enough for Agatha Christie to write twelve short stories about the adventures of Mr. Pyne in 1932.

Mr. Pyne is not a detective in the usual sense. He says, in fact: "I stand in the place of the doctor.... But ... if I undertake a case. the cure is practically guaranteed."

Mr. Pyne spent thirty-five years of his life compiling statistics in a government office. After his retirement, he decided to use his experience in a unique manner. "Unhappiness," says Mr. Pyne, "can be classified under five main heads—no more.... Once you know the cause of a malady, the remedy should not be impossible."

Perhaps most people come to see Parker Pyne on a lark, but they are so impressed by his sympathetic manner that they usually hire him to make them happy.

The sight of Parker Pyne is reassuring. He is a large man, not necessarily fat, with a nobly proportioned bald head. Behind strong glasses, his little eyes twinkle. He is just the person to inspire confidence. And well he should, since he always makes good his boast to make you happy or refund your fee. For the retired soldier, he finds excitement and a lovely wife thrown in the bargain. To a neglected wife, he returns the husband. If a man's wife has strayed, he gets her back. But the man now wants another, a dilemma for Mr. Pyne: should he return the fee?

We are treated to only a few of Mr. Pyne's unique solutions, since Mrs. Christie does not write of him again. It was probably the cost of those advertisements.

Mr. Satterthwaite and Mr. Quin

In 1930, Mrs. Christie had two gentlemen work in fairly close association to solve the problems of those few who were troubled in the English upper class. There were twelve such persons in that economically depressed year. Their troubles were not what one would call financial, unless the stake of your own life on the turn of the roulette wheel could be called a monetary problem. (Only the very rich have financial problems at the roulette table.)

A man is troubled by the thought that his wife may be a murderess. Harley Quin appears and solves the problem. He is unlike any of Mrs. Christie's other characters in that he possesses a definite supernatural aura. A tall, slender man with a deep, steady, melodious voice, he arrives and leaves mysteriously in a rainbow of color that ripples over him. When he has gone, the problem is solved.

Mr. Satterthwaite is a sixty-two at the time of the tale. He is a small, bent, dried-up man with an elfin face, peering eyes, and an intense interest in other people's business. He often just happens to be on the scene when Mr. Quin arrives, and he revels in the spectacle. After some chance meetings, Mr. Satterthwaite comes to expect his appearance as we learn in the *Mysterious Mr. Quin*:

> Tall, dark, smiling, the familiar figure of Mr. Quin rose from the table ... the well-rembered voice spoke.
>
> "Ah! Mr. Satterthwaite, we meet again. An unexpected meeting ... I assure you that I have not a bowl of goldfish or a rabbit to produce from my sleeve."
>
> "Too bad," cried Mr. Satterthwaite, "Yes, I must confess—I do rather adopt that attitude toward you. A man of magic."

Mrs. Christie was making no more magic, however, and Mr. Satterthwaite and Mr. Quin teamed up no more.

Chapter IX

Dame Agatha's Puzzles

It is a smooth, worn mahogany ledge as wide as a garden bench. It sits along the sharply sloping sides of a Victorian bathtub. The ledge is laden with the cores of gnawed apples. There is a splash in the tub. Dame Agatha Christie is working.

Actual writing time at her typewriter or at a tape recorder is anywhere from six weeks to three months for the at least yearly Christie thriller. But most of the work is done in the tub, figuring those intricately misleading puzzles that have stumped mystery buffs for more than fifty years.

The puzzle prestidigitator operates on a principle that every nightclub magician knows—misdirection. Has the date been removed from the calendar since the murder, Poirot queries the butler? The butler walks across the room, looks at the calendar, and replies. You triumphantly remember "dates"—and totally miss the point, but M. Poirot has found that the butler is too nearsighted to see across the room—a fact that is of utmost importance to the plot.

In Francis Wyndham's article in *The London Sunday Times*, he commented: "Agatha Christie writes animated algebra. She dares us to solve a basic equation buried beneath a proliferation of irrelevancies. By the last page, or final curtain, everything should have been eliminated except for the motive and identity of the murderer: the elaborate working-out, apparently too complicated to grasp, is suddenly reduced to satisfactory simplicity. The effect is one of comfortable catharsis."

Of her own work, Dame Agatha says: "All my early books were very conventional. They were unnecessarily complicated with quantities of clues and subplots. Stupid policemen were dragged in, and I felt I had to have a detective and a Watson. . . . When I re-read those first ones I'm amazed at the amount of servants drifting about. And nobody is really doing any work. They're always having tea on the lawn like in E.F. Benson. It gives one great nostalgia for the past.

"But the one thing that infuriates me is when people complain that I always set my books in country houses. You *have* to be concerned with a house; with where people *live*. You can make it a hotel, or a train, or a pub—but it's got to be where people are brought together. And I think it must be a background that readers will recognize, because explanations are so boring. If you set a detective story in, say, a laboratory, I don't think people would enjoy it so much. No, a country house is obviously the best."

Her characters are doctors, lawyers, top military men, and clergymen—the people who tenant the quiet and comfortable upper-class background in which she herself has always lived. Even her villains are somehow respectable, and there are all those big, gracious country houses. "I could never manage miners talking in pubs, because I don't know what miners talk about in pubs," she says.

The solutions to her puzzles are human solutions. They lie in the basics of human nature. There is no secret decoder ring, no multipurpose attache case. Nor do her detectives know the identity of 182 different sorts of tobacco ash or exactly where, throughout the British Isles, each type of soil is to be found. What they *do* know is the psychology of human behavior.

Perhaps the entire means of Agatha Christie's method of detection can be summed up in just one of her sentences. In *The ABC Murders*, Hercule Poirot states: *"When I know what the murderer is like, I shall be able to find out who he is."* The italics are Poirot's.

By sticking to the timeless methods of detection, that is, psychological ones, Christie's detectives bid fair to outlive even those of Poe and Conan Doyle in the public affection. We are no longer impressed by Holmes' rather rudimentary chemical skills or his ability to deceive criminals by playing phonograph records. Nor are we much interested in cryptographical decoding in this age of computers. But Miss Marple's uncanny ability to read human nature and Poirot's skill at finding the hidden truths in obvious things will always be virtues of human life.

It is for this reason that the Detection Club Oath bids members, "Observe a seemly moderation in the use of Gangs, Conspiracies, Death-Rays, Ghosts, Hypnotism, Trap-Doors, Chinamen, Super-Criminals and Lunatics; and utterly and forever to forswear Mysterious Poisons unknown to Science." In other words, the good mysteries are those that reveal their solutions in human rather than mechanical terms.

The Detection Club is a world-reknowned guild of mystery writers founded by Anthony Berkeley and based in London. At least one of the obligations imposed on its members by the Club seems to present no problem for Mrs. Christie—that of honoring the Queen's English. She may not be a creator of the sort of prose that would satisfy Edmund Wilson, but in sheer readability she has an almost perfect score. While not a scholarly writer by any means, Christie displays an easy familiarity with the classics of English literature, notably the King James Bible and Shakespeare.

Agatha Christie's daughter, Rosalind, was named, as were many of her mother's books and characters, after a Shakespearean lady. Rosalind, herself now old enough to be a grandmother, has remained close to her mother, and Mrs. Christie claims that her daughter guesses the solution to all her mysteries before finishing the book.

Among Christie's most famous Shakespearean titles are *Murder Most Foul*, *By the Pricking of My Thumbs*, and, of course, *The Mousetrap*, which is the name of the aborted theatrical presented by Hamlet to his mother's court in hope of ensnaring his father's murderer.

The original inspiration for Mrs. Christie's phenomenally long-running play was a short story of hers entitled *Three Blind Mice*, which points up the interesting fact that by far the most common literary source for an Agatha

Christie mystery is the English nursery rhyme. In the case of rhymes, she uses not only single lines as titles, but often bases whole plots on the movement of the poem; this occurred most completely in the often-filmed *Ten Little Indians*. Besides this rhyme, she has used *Sing a Song of Sixpence; Hickory Dickory Dock; A Pocket Full of Rye; One, Two, Buckle My Shoe* (published in America as *The Patriotic Murders); There was a Crooked Man; This Little Piggy* (under the English title *Five Little Pigs);* and *Three Blind Mice.*

It is not uncommon for mystery story writers to insert literary references into their work or to suggest that their detectives, even the most hard-boiled of them, have more knowledge of culture than they often let on. Hercule Poirot, for instance, seems to have near-perfect command of English, when he wants to. Miss Marple, like her creator, is well-versed in the classics, as well as English flower-and-folk lore. Lew Archer is known to wax uncharacteristically philosophical toward the end of every case, and the culture of Sherlock Holmes and his brother, Mycroft, is legendary. Even Agatha Christie's lesser-known detectives, such as the mystery writer Ariadne Oliver, show classical reference. In Greek mythology, Ariadne, the daughter of Minos, gave Theseus a clue of thread, from which that most important element in the modern mystery story receives its name. Christie's other classically named sleuth, Hercule Poirot, has been set by his creator as was the mythological Hercules, to perform twelve difficult tasks in the short story collection *The Labors of Hercules*.

No one would claim that classical references and a passing acquaintance with Shakespeare make for great literature, but it's clear that detective fiction has always attracted clever, well-educated writers. Many of these have insisted over the years that mysteries are, indeed, legitimate literary forms, at least as legitimate as that eighteenth-century latecomer, the novel. Some partisans of the genre insist that when another century has gone by, scholars will be poking as eagerly into the roots of the mystery as they are now working at digging up the history of the novel. Whether or not this will come to pass, it must be clear by now that the mystery is a respectable form of literature—light literature, if you like—with its own rules and organizational necessities and its own set of critical criteria.

What sort of mystery does Dame Agatha prefer? "Give me a murder in quiet family surroundings," she says, "the kind you read about in the papers—not the explosive, gangster type." Here are fifty-five of the kind of mystery that Agatha Christie enjoys most. She ought to—she wrote all of them.

The Mysterious Affairs at Styles (1920). Critics say it was a noble maiden effort springing from a great fondness for the mold formed by Conan Doyle: the eccentric and brilliant detective with a suitably idiotic friend. It marks the beginning of Hercule Poirot's career.

The Secret Adversary (1922). Tommy and Tuppence meet after the war to track down a master criminal. Incidentally, they posted the banns, beginning a happy marriage and partnership that has lasted fifty-one years so far.

Murder on the Links (1923). Hastings is "Watson," telling us of Poirot's solution in the case. The murderer, in a fit of pique against the national game, does away with his victim on the golf links.

The Man in the Brown Suit (1924). Here is another supercriminal who brings about the death of a man by electrocution in a London subway station. The smell of mothballs takes Anne Beddingfield on a thrilling adventure. The last stop is not in the subway but in Africa.

The Secret of Chimneys (1925). Superintendent Battle proves that the police are not as stupid as some mystery writers would make them. The plot and characters are complicated and involved but Battle, with the help of the charming scoundrel, Anthony Cade, solves the case.

The Murder of Roger Ackroyd (1926). The great classic that brought Agatha Christie success. The surprise ending is still a sore point among students of the genre. This is the ultimate Christie. Agatha Christie says, "I have a certain amount of rules. No false words must be uttered by me. To write: 'Mrs. Armstrong walked home wondering who had committed the murder,' would be unfair if she had done it herself. But it's not unfair to leave things out. In *Roger Ackroyd* I made the narrator write: 'I left ten minutes later, having done everything I needed to do.' There's lack of explanation there, but no false statement."

The Big Four (1927). Hastings and Poirot are together again in a novel that originally was four separate short stories. The stories are held together by the device of a four-member cabal that plots the domination of the world. The story of Achille Poirot is included in this novel.

Mystery of the Blue Train (1928). Agatha Christie says, "Easily the worst book I ever wrote was the *Mystery of the Blue Train.* I hate it. It's neither one thing or the other." But if you're interested in a description of luxury travel on the Riviera in the 1920s, get on the Blue Train anyway.

The Seven Dials Mystery (1929). Seven Dials is a secret organization that took its name from the famous London district. But the mystery takes place at Chimneys, the estate that figured in the 1925 novel. The Marquis of Caterham and his daughter, Lady Eileen, figure in the case.

Partners in Crime (1929). Mrs. Christie uses Tommy and Tuppence to spoof the master detective Hercule Poirot. " 'Let us arrange our facts neatly, and with method ... and now what significant fact strikes us?' There was a pause, no significant fact striking either of them."

Murder at the Vicarage (1930). We make our first trip to St. Mary Mead and meet for the first time Miss Jane Marple. A local misogynist is murdered. Nobody really misses him, but Miss Marple finds the murderer anyhow.

Peril at End House (1932). Poirot has no Watson against whom to display his brilliance; he almost falls into a trap set by a very dangerous lady.

Lord Edgware Dies (1933). American title: *Thirteen at Dinner.* One of the best and most famous of the early Christie books. Lady Edgware seems to perform the impossible, but gossip from across the Channel helps Poirot solve the mystery.

Murder on the Orient Express (1934). American title: *Murder in the Calais Coach. Time Magazine,* March 5, 1934, said: "Basing the tale on America's great kidnapping, the author brings the arch criminal on a snow-bound Jugoslavian express. Coincidentally, the rotund, penetrating Poirot is aboard. Clues abound. Alibis are frequent and unassailable. But nothing confounds the great Hercule who, after propounding alternative solutions to his jury of two, retires modestly."

Three-Act Tragedy (1935). American title: *Murder in Three Acts.* Mrs. Christie takes Hercule Poirot into the world of the theater, where the murder is more than a rehearsal. The danger to Poirot is real and not part of the play.

Death in the Clouds (1935). American title: *Death in the Air*. The old closed-room puzzle brought up to date in the air. How was it done? Poirot solves the case.

The ABC Murders (1935). Is he a madman or a cunning criminal? This popular classic has intrigued mystery buffs for years. The murders are announced in advance and in alphabetical order. The recent French film thriller, *The Sleeping Car Murders*, utilized the same plot device without benefit of Mrs. Christie's skill.

Murder in Mesopotamia (1936). Poirot retraces the steps taken by Professor Max Mallowan and his wife, Agatha Christie. Archeology, espionage, and murder make up the plot.

Cards on the Table (1936). Agatha Christie says, "Quite good, the bridge one, an interesting technique. Keeping the interest divided between only three people and still making the end a surprise, quite difficult to do."

Dumb Witness (1937). American title: *Poirot Loses a Client*. Hastings is back and bumbling around. Poirot receives a letter. Miss Arundell writes, saying she fears for her life. But she has been dead for two months.

True brings low tar and low nicotine to the 100mm smoker.
True 100's.

100's Regular and 100's Menthol:
12 mg. "tar", 0.7 mg. nicotine,
av. per cigarette, by FTC method.

Warning: The Surgeon General Has Determined That Cigarette Smoking Is Dangerous to Your Health.

© Lorillard 1975

True Menthol brings low tar and low nicotine to the 100mm smoker.

True Menthol 100's.

100's Regular and 100's Menthol:
12 mg. "tar", 0.7 mg. nicotine,
av. per cigarette, by FTC method.

Warning: The Surgeon General Has Determined That Cigarette Smoking Is Dangerous to Your Health.

© Lorillard 1975

Death on the Nile (1937). Agatha Christie says she likes this one best of all her foreign travel books: "The three characters . . . seem to me to be real and alive."

Hercule Poirot's Christmas (1938). American titles: *Murder for Christmas; A Holiday for Murder.* The family gathers around the tree when Simeon Lee, a millionaire, invites them for a holiday of torment. One of his offspring decides to do him in. Poirot interrupts his holiday to solve the murder.

Appointment with Death (1938). An American family travels through the Holy Land and the trip is anything but a pilgrimage. Poirot gets them on their way again.

Murder Is Easy (1939). American title: *Easy to Kill.* On her way to Scotland Yard to report on strange deaths in her town, a lady is run down and killed. Luke Fitz-William and Superintendent Battle solve the case and arrest the murderer.

Ten Little Niggers (1939). American titles: *And Then There Were None; Ten Little Indians; The Nursery Rhyme Murders. Time Magazine,* March 4, 1940 said: "One of the most ingenious thrillers in many a day. A shadowy host collects ten people, each with an unpunished past, on a small island off the English coast. There the nursery rhyme about the ten little Indians, ghoulishly revised to fit the gathering, is remorselessly fulfilled."

Sad Cypress (1940). According to Agatha Christie, "*Sad Cypress* could have been good, but it was quite ruined by having Poirot in it. I always thought *something* was wrong with it but didn't discover what until I read it again sometime after."

One, Two, Buckle My Shoe (1940). American title: *The Patriotic Murders.* Another nursery-rhyme thriller from Dame Agatha. This time the murder allows Hercule Poirot to escape his dentist—who is the victim.

Evil Under the Sun (1941). Everyone at a seaside resort in Devon comes under suspicion in this love-generated murder mystery—even the victim.

N or M? (1941). Tommy and Tuppence Beresford are aging, but still have enough spunk to catch German spies in England. They prove they are not too old to be useful to their son, Derek, the RAF lieutenant.

The Body in the Library (1942). "This is the best first chapter I have ever written," says Agatha Christie. The book opens: "Wake up, Arthur ... you've got to listen. Mary came in and said there was a body in the library."

Five Little Pigs (1943). American title: *Murder in Retrospect*. The trail is not fresh; the murder is sixteen years old. But Poirot investigates and clears the victim's wife. He also finds the real murderer.

The Moving Finger (1943). Agatha Christie comments, *"The Moving Finger* had good misdirection. There is a trap set at the very beginning and, as arranged by the murderer, you fall right in it." The anonymous letters are vicious, accusing just about every one. Before Miss Marple can put a stop to the letters, murder is committed. Through the post she tracks the murderer.

Towards Zero (1944). American title: *Come and Be Hanged*. The murder almost comes off but Superintendent Battle muddles through and winds up an extremely complicated plot.

Death Comes as the End (1945). The trail of this murder would really be too stale for Hercule Poirot. It takes place in the Middle Kingdom of Egypt three thousand years ago. Mrs. Christie shows that human nature does not change. She commented, "Practically all the questions, especially the most trivial, required a lot of research to answer."

Sparkling Cyanide (1945). American title: *Remembered Death.* Mrs. Christie, who is always happiest with a phial in her hand, has good reason to be happy about this one. The death-dealing cyanide is administered in a bottle of champagne.

The Hollow (1946). American title: *Murder After Hours.* A difficult case for Poirot, who cannot put his finger on the psychology of the person he seeks. It is because that mind is creative rather than destructive.

The Labors of Hercules (1947). Poirot is confronted with the twelve labors from the cleaning of the Agean stables to the capture of the Nemean lion and the hound of Cerberus. On the way he meets an old love.

Taken at the Flood (1948). American title: *There Is a Tide.* There is a rich young widow and her in-laws, and soon there is one murder and then another. Poirot undoes the mystery and rolls back the tide.

Crooked House (1949). Dame Agatha says, "Yes, *Crooked House* is one of my favorites. But I had difficulty with that one. The publishers wanted me to change the end—but that's how I'd written it, and some things you can't change."

Endless Night (1957). Agatha Christie says, "Usually I spend three to four months on a book, but I wrote *Endless Night* in six weeks. If I can write fairly quickly, the result is more spontaneous." This is a sinister drama based on the legend of Gipsy's Acre. A monstrous crime is revealed.

A Murder is Announced (1950). The year is '50 and the book is 50. Agatha Christie's fiftieth murder has Miss Marple taking up ventriloquism. Her fiftieth mystery was the occasion for outpourings of praise throughout the British Empire and in the Colonies—American included. Prime Minister Clement Atlee took time out from matters of Sate to laud his "favorite writer."

They Came to Baghdad (1951). Mrs. Mallowan again in the digs bringing us a mystery made up of two parts archeology, one part romance, and three parts of the British Secret Service.

They Do It With Mirrors (1952). American title: *Murder with Mirrors*. Miss Marple is brought into the case by Mrs. van Rydock who has grave concern for her sister. Not to worry, Jane Marple is on the job, solves all problems and the murder as well.

Mrs. McGinty's Dead (1952). Why should a charwoman, Mrs. McGinty, have been murdered? Poirot's puzzles it out. There's intrique and an intriquing photograph. This book was certainly not one of Mrs. Christie's favorites after it was filmed. Poirot magically became Miss Marple and the title was changed to *Murder Most Foul*.

A Pocket Full of Rye (1953). The nursery rhyme occasions three murders. The king is done in in his counting house, his queen while eating bread and honey, and the maid has a clothespin on her nose. Miss Marple shows up at the family manse to solve the triple killing. Her best line, "But what I mean to say is: have you gone in to the question of blackbirds."

After the Funeral (1953). American title: *Funerals are Fatal*. Mrs. Christie vexed again. The movie, called *Murder at the Gallop*, once more substituted Miss Marple for the true hero of the case, Hercule Poirot. There are deaths in the Abernathie family, but the little Belgian muddles through and family pictures help him solve the case.

Destination Unknown (1954). American title: *So Many Steps to Death*. Rick's Cafe has gone and nobody sings *As Time Goes By*, but the setting is Casablanca all the same. An atomic scientist defects—the wrong way—and a young redhead wants to do herself in. It comes out all right at the end.

4:50 from Paddington (1957). American titles: *What Mrs. McGillicuddy Saw!* and *Murder She Said*. It's the trains passing in the night gambit when Miss Marple's friend, Mrs. McGillicuddy, sees murder committed before her eyes. Both the victim and the murderer must be tracked down and Miss Marple is up to it in her usual style.

Cat Among the Pigeons (1959). There's a month of murder and kidnapping at an exclusive English girls' boarding school. Poirot, towering above the little ladies, finds the jewels in a tennis racket and wraps up the murderer in a net.

The Pale Horse (1961). Mrs. Oliver is her usual whimsical self, but she provides the clue that helps Inspector Lejeune trap the murder. This is the novel that caught a real murderer when a famous London forensic specialist remembered the denouement and put the police on the trail of mass-poisoner Frederick Graham Young.

The Clocks (1963). Poirot discusses his famous counterparts and muses on the mystery. A second plot involves Colin Lamb, who refuses to capitalize on his father's famous name and so keeps it concealed. Mrs. Christie thinks his father may be Superintendent Battle.

At Bertram's Hotel (1965). In a mood for reminiscence, Miss Marple revisits a quaint Edwardian hotel. With the sage of St. Mary Mead on the scene there is, naturally, a murder. Miss Marple solves the murder and decides that you cannot relive your past.

Third Girl (1967). A young girl can not remember committing murder, but finds herself with a compelling motive and a blood-stained knife. She seeks help from Poirot, but when she sees him says, "You're too old. I'm really very sorry." Poirot says, "Nom d'un nom d'un nom . . ." He enlists the aid of Mrs. Ariadne Oliver who seems to be more concerned with her wallpaper than Poirot's advancing age.

Elephants Can Remember (1972). Hercule Poirot and Adriadne Oliver team up again to follow a stale trail of the murderer of a long-dead victim. The trail connects to a plot that threatens to destroy a beautiful young girl.

Postern of Fate (1973). Tommy and Tuppence are back again. Young in heart and mind but the legs are getting old. The clues range from *Black Arrow* to Cain and Abel to Gallant Truelove. Tommy and Tuppence are not saving the Empire anymore and the youthful zeal is gone, but they're "a gifted pair," all the same.

Chapter X

But Is It Art?

As Ellery Queen has said, the first murder story was the tale of Cain and Abel, making violent crime in literature as old as literature itself. But Genesis does not contain the first mystery story, for the simple reason that there is no detective in the Bible. True detective fiction had to wait for Poe's creation of Inspector Dupin, the character who ties it all together.

It is in the personality and the analytic faculties of the detective that all knots are untied, all puzzles solved. It is he or, just as often, she who carries the ball of colored yarn through the maze, trailing a string for the reader to follow. The detective stands for the reader himself, poking his nose into hidden corners, finding out what the reader wants to know.

The calendar of mystery fiction began in 1841. In that year, Edgar Allen Poe published *The Murders in the Rue Morgue*, in which, if you recall, the villain turned out to be an orangutan. It is now generally accepted that *Murders* was the first modern detective story, and the haunted Poe has been credited as the inventor of the form. Thus, detective fiction was born in an atmosphere of literacy, intellectual curiosity, and scientific inquiry. Ever since, mysteries have been serious business to their writers and readers alike. But critical approval was far behind popular acceptance.

There have been notable exceptions: in this century, Jacques Barzun, Joseph Wood Krutch, Somerset Maugham, and Bernard DeVoto, all known for their attentiveness to "real" literature, have commented favorably on the detective story. Mystery readers can count among their number such literary figures Andre Gide, not to mention Woodrow Wilson and John F. Kennedy, who, if not actually literary lights, were nevertheless serious men.

Even the irascible Edmund Wilson, who never met a mystery story he liked after Sherlock Holmes, was moved in 1943 to express his irritation with the form in an essay he wrote for *The New Yorker*, thereby adding stature to the object of his distaste. In his essay *Who Cares Who Killed Roger Ackroyd?*, Wilson claimed that detective fiction could never be real literature and, having passed this judgment, he dismissed mystery fiction as ipso facto worthless. "We shall do well," he said, "to discourage the squandering of this paper (the wartime paper-saving drive was on) which might be put to better use."

In fact, the mystery story or novel is both less and more than real literature. True, most characters are two-dimensional. Hercule Poirot, Agatha Christie's "Sherlock" figure, is really a kind of cartoon Frenchman, although she insists that he is Belgian. It is also true that, as Wilson pointed out in despair, many mysteries are occupied with minute turns of phrase, details, timetables, and other technicalities, such as interior maps of vast mansions drawn to scale. Wilson was bored to the point of dozing by Dorothy Sayers' encyclopedic knowledge of bell-ringing in *The Nine Tailors*, considered by many devotees of the mystery novel as a sublime example of perfection. Nor was the venerable critic any happier about the *writing* of some mystery writers, describing the much loved Ngaio Marsh as a producer of "unappetizing sawdust."

Wilson and other critics also downgraded mysteries for their rigid format, calling them "formula" stories, as if writing within prescribed limitations were an inferior art. Since nobody has ever said the same of sonneteers or makers of sestinas, the comment can be dismissed as pure prejudice. In fact, it is a great challenge to an author to obey all or at least most of the rules and still produce tantalizing fiction.

Given its restrictions, detective fiction can be admired according to its own standards. The idea of writing a new detective novel is not to ring changes on the Great Theme of Life, but on the smaller, more circumscribed theme of the *puzzle* of life.

Detective stories reduce even the most atrocious crimes to games, bringing order out of chaos. Nothing happens without a reason, and the mystery's vast appeal lies precisely in this mechanism. It is against all the rules for the murder to have been committed randomly, by accident, or for no reason. There is always a motive, perfectly logical and inevitable once we see it.

The reader "escapes" into the detective story, where nothing is impossible to solve and where the unfathomable can be explained by logical thinking. In a world whose every tendency is to greater and greater disorder, we are profoundly soothed by this sort of perfect explanation for terrible deeds. The effect is further enhanced, particularly by wry, somewhat detached writers like Agatha Christie, because of the attitude the detective takes toward homicide. To Hercule Poirot or Miss Marple or even Tommy and Tuppence Beresford, murder is so matter-of-fact, so interesting; a fascinating puzzle to be worked out much like a picture puzzle on one's game table in the drawing room. All fears are dispelled and all questions are answered.

The idea of the mystery story is supremely simple. The reader is presented with a seemingly inexplicable crime, almost always murder. He tries to guess the explanation. The author's task is to provide the most ingenious answer possible, consistent with all the clues, but unguessed by the reader until it is revealed. The paradox for the habitual mystery reader is that he wants to guess the answer but will be disappointed if he does. He demands that the writer fool him, but at the same time he wants a fair chance at the secret.

The reader is disappointed—outraged, in fact—if he discovers at the end that he was not given some vital clue. The detective is never permitted to discover a clue offstage where the reader cannot watch. The reader doesn't care in the least how many red herrings the author throws at him, as long as the real fish are there somewhere.

Nor may the solution come from supernatural sources, intuition, lucky guesses, funny feelings or that old investigator's "hunch" that just happens to be right. The crime must be solved by logical means; deduced from the evidence at hand in just the same scientific manner that interested Dupin and Sherlock Holmes. This does not preclude the use of psychology under the heading of "science." Many of the best mysteries are solved because of the detective's inherent sense of human understanding. He may feel that a character cannot have committed a murder because of something he, the detective, understands about the character's personality. It is, however, an established ground rule that neither murderer nor detective can receive help from Martians, spirits, unheard-of poisons or devices, teleportation, or the Mafia.

Furthermore, the crime must be a domestic one. Assignation and international intrigue, except perhaps as atmosphere, have no place in the proper mystery. It can be murder for profit or revenge or madness or passion, but no love interest or character development should be allowed to loom so large that it overshadows the basic puzzle.

The mystery reader also demands a well-made plot. Each entrance and exit, each cryptic line from every lying mouth must make sense in light of the explanation that finally comes. Does a lawyer recognize a disguised witness by the characteristic movement of her hands (*Witness for the Prosecution*)? If the author did not mention that little habit in another scene in the story, the reader will claim foul. But the author, who is Agatha Christie, knows the rules better than most. After checking back through the book, the reader must admit that he was bested in a fair contest. This kind of dependability is what makes Agatha Christie so everlastingly popular.

The mystery audience prefers a Byzantine labyrinth for a story line, complete with false trails, chance encounters, and amazing coincidences. Agatha Christie can produce this kind of plot, if not effortlessly, then at least in incredible abundance. Even her shortest short stories have turns and counter-turns crammed into a few pages.

The plot density of *Witness for the Prosecution*, for instance, allowed it to be expanded from a story of some twenty pages to a fulllength play with no loss of essence. Christie's play, *Love From a Stranger*, which has been filmed twice, was taken from her short psychological thriller, *Philomel Cottage*.

Like Poe and Conan Doyle, Agatha Christie is a "head" writer, so familiar with all the rules and tricks of mystery stories that she even knows how to violate the conventions and get away with it. Her most notorious violation, *The Murder of Roger Ackroyd*, is discussed in an earlier chapter. Nevertheless, her crimes are always real crimes—not accidents, suicides, or dreams—and the solution to the mystery is always there, in plain sight, for the discovery of the clever reader.

Since the genre requires that the clues be laid out, some readers do guess the answer before the end of the story. But, if the writer has been ingenious and true to the psychological situations he or she has established, this is not grounds for criticism. One can only be offended if he spots an old, tired device. It is simply not fair to trot out the old look-alike villain (perhaps the twin of the innocent suspect), the tell-tale cigar stub of a brand smoked only by one person in the Western world, or the watchdog who doesn't bark at the intruder because he is familiar. Neither is it fair to reuse a famous device, no matter how clever. There can be only one mystery which is solved by a "society of mystery writers," that one, *The Poisoned Chocolates Case*, was written forty years ago by Anthony Berkeley.

Berkeley, who also wrote as Francis Iles, was the founder of the London Detection Club, just the sort of mystery writers' guild that figures in his classic mystery. Members of the club include the cream of British detective story writers, which is to say, the cream of the genre throughout the world. It is the members of the guild who have evolved the "rules" of the game. Mrs. Christie is a member, as was her friend and highly acclaimed contemporary, Dorothy Sayers. Between them they helped mold a somewhat loose art form into a concrete shape and give it life and a tradition. If Dorothy Sayers has presented the detective story with literary distinction, Agatha Christie has kept its hair short and its feet on the ground.

According to Dorothy Sayers, it was no accident that the fullest flowering of the detective story took place in England. In all the world, no people are more attached to the notion of fair play—for criminal and cop alike—than are the English. And none are less afraid of their police.

It was only a matter of time until a detective appeared who embraced all the principles of honesty, doggedness, and humanitarianism which Englishmen had come to associate with Scotland Yard. Conan Doyle introduced him when he published *A Study in Scarlet* in 1887; he was an overnight sensation. The literature of Sherlock Holmes began to arrive in installments immediately thereafter, focusing good English common sense and ethical conduct in the eccentric person of one brilliant detective.

The idea of a supersleuth, someone even more devoted to the truth than the police and even better at finding it, was not new. Poe's detective Dupin had also one-upped the police with his careful observation and quiet logic. The mystery story genre, from its inception to the present day, has always reflected the anti-authoritarian bias of the Anglo-American mind. Even if the police are the good guys, no official force can do the job as well as a knight errant, a single brilliant individual whose logical mind cuts through all the bureaucratic pudding and goes to the hard stuff at once. The Scotland Yard inspectors, superintendents, and detectives come under the heading of private individuals, inasmuch as they are often at odds with local police when solving a crime.

It should be noted, however, that, except for Poirot, the ex-policeman, and Superintendent Battle, all of Mrs. Christie's detectives are amateurs. They are often drawn into working with the police—they are well-known, after all—but they are not professionals like Dupin or superprofessionals like Sherlock Holmes. This insistence on the competence of ordinary citizens is uniquely English. It survives there even more than in America, where we have gone in for the "hard-boiled" detective, usually a former cop, who knows all the inside tricks the cops know and then some.

G.K. Chesterton, the first president of the London Detection Club and creator of the Father Brown detective stories, insisted that there was poetry in mysteries. To him, the mystery was a Romance of Civilization, a way of seeing the possiblities in the common environment of modern man. "No one can have failed to notice," Chesterton said, "that in these stories the hero or the investigator crosses London with something of the loneliness and liberty of a prince in a tale of elfland, that in the course of that incalcuable journey the casual omnibus assumes the primal colours of a fairy ship."

Agatha Christie has certainly contributed her share to the romance of London, not to mention the country cottage, the manor house, and the quaint village. More than anything else, Dame Agatha is English. Her novels and stories over the years are a chronicle of her own growth and of changes in the world.

They are also a history of the evolution of a certain class of English life. The fact that it is the upper class has at least a little to do with the lady's lasting popularity. People are fascinated by the nobility as such, as the Greeks recognized when they insisted that tragedies should be about people of high birth. The things that Christie characters do—including digging in the Mesopotamian ruins and going on tours to the Caribbean—are activities that are inaccessible to most of her readers. They paint a picture of a lifestyle that is more graceful than any we have today. It is a style that Agatha Christie has known, one that is passing away before her eyes.

Anyone who has lived as long as Mrs. Christie is bound to have a strong sense of the ways in which the conventions of society have altered, and the directions these changes have taken. But few people, no matter how old they are, have managed to provide us with such a casual and undidactic record, written and preserved for all to see, as has Agatha Christie. We have heard a lot, perhaps too much, about the repression and narrowness of the Edwardian period. But Agatha Christie makes a good case for the value of at least some of the old ways. Like Miss Marple, she hates to see the world change, though she's not too old to see that some of the changes are for the best.

Mysteries in the Christie style are, in fact, romantic. The Queen of Crime introduces us to people that most of us don't know in real life: fabulously wealthy old ladies; great (and rich) men of science and law; foreign actresses, knights, and ladies; and the picturesque old family retainers who serve them. These characters are her intimates, drawn from her life.

Added to this rich scheme of things are Christie's middle-class detectives. Eccentric though they may be, they are not loners living apart from the warmth of human companionship. Miss Jane Marple, who almost never leaves St. Mary Mead, solves the most depraved murders with what can only be described as housewifely methods—the recollection of old nursery rhymes and the comparison of the great of the world to her fellow villagers and their homely life.

If the big-city detectives are knights errant, Miss Marple is a kind of Fairy Queen of the Everyday, whose little village-bred store of psychological truths is adequate to any occasion. Like Chesterton, Agatha Christie considers it a positive thing to see poetry in our ordinary lives.

Contrast this to the American detectives of the hard-boiled type. Unlike Miss Marple or the Beresfords, Mike Hammer, Sam Spade, and Lew Archer are lonely outsiders. They lead, to paraphrase Thoreau, lives of quiet desperation; holding things together, yes, but just barely. Lew Archer drives through the network of Los Angeles freeways, going days without sleep and many hours between roadhouse steaks to find the answer he knows is there. Nevertheless, both he and the reader have the sense that this solution means only a brief pause before Archer will be compelled to jump back into the car, trying to tie up the unraveling universe all over again.

Mrs. Christie's sleuths, on the other hand,

simply radiate satisfaction once the mystery is cleared up. Poirot can retire to polish his ego in peace; Miss Marple, with relief, can hurry back to St. Mary Mead, where a sense of order and calm prevail. All's right with the world, at least until the next Agatha Christie book comes out. This view is a comforting one, suggesting that society is pretty much all right as presently constituted, that it can be patched up where it has begun to crack, and that there are several brainy ladies and gentlemen of good will still around to attend to the patching.

Those who prefer the Dashiell Hammett or Ross MacDonald kind of detective on the grounds that he is more "realistic" are ignoring the extent to which Mrs. Christie reports on what she sees. True enough, not everyone lives as her people do—not any more. But there are some, there were more once, and there is still something the rest of us can learn from the representation of their way of life. The work of Agatha Christie, taken as a whole, presents a picture, idealized, to be sure, of the life and work of a whole class of people during the last seventy-five years.

Is it art? Perhaps not. But it is true that, despite Edmund Wilson's protests, the narrow demands of the mystery form do not preclude the creation of "great" literature in this genre. Opinions vary, but almost everyone thinks there have been at least one or two mystery writers who qualify as "literary." Raymond Chandler is one major candidate; Dashiell Hammett comes in for a great deal of literary approval, and Ross MacDonald gets front-page reviews in *The New York Times Book Review*, which is about the best any novelist can hope for these days. And, of course, everybody agrees that Poe and Conan Doyle are masters of the mystery realm.

There has always been hot debate over whether James' *The Turn of the Screw* is actually a mystery story, but no one would deny that Faulkner's masterly short story, *The Six Stories of Knights Gambit*, (1949) is indeed an example of the genre, complete with detective and narrator. The story alone proves that a great writer can transcend all imposed limitations of form.

But even Agatha Christie's staunchest admirers do not claim that she writes like Henry James or William Faulkner. They say only that what she does is worth doing and that she does it extremely well.

If her creation of characters cannot be compared to that of the great novelists, she has, in her own way, given life to several memorable persons. Miss Marple and Mrs. Oliver and Parker Pyne and the Beresfords and Hercule Poirot are as familiar to us as our own relatives, and probably a lot more fun. Mystery readers have come to feel they know such characters because they appear so consistently the very same, year after year and novel after novel. They may or may not age, as Mrs. Christie dictates. Hercule Poirot, for example, must be at least 135 years old by now, having "retired" from police work in 1904, but you would never know it. He goes on, solving crimes and fiddling with his moustaches. It is this kind of lifelong predictability that we are attracted to.

Miss Marple is, of course, now thoroughly confused in the public mind, both with Agatha Christie herself and with Margaret Rutherford, who played the role in several films. She has, in effect, a life of her own—not the worst fate an author could wish for her characters.

The case of Agatha Christie is more than a little like one of her own mysteries. It is no wonder that she knows so well how to veil and conceal, how to hold the answer until the very last. Her own personal life has been as secretive as that of any public figure in modern times. In Agatha Christie's case, there is no public life, except for the books themselves.

What is clear about the Duchess of Death is that, in spite of her preoccupation with crime and murder, she is essentially an optimist, a survivor whose sympathies are all on the side of the living. It helps to explain why such great

masses of people the world over will buy anything at all by Agatha Christie. Whatever her
faults, she can be relied on not to let down in
this most essential aspect of the craft. If anyone should hold it against detective stories that
they aim to soothe, let it be remembered that
this really the aim of all art; to give us some
comfort by helping us to comprehend, to mentally master what we can never get the best of
physically. Mystery stories, like chess, are
small, self-contained worlds where unique laws
obtain. We would never think of faulting chess
because it isn't very much like the real world,
why should we do so for the murder mystery?

Chapter XI

Challengers And Champions;
Christie's Critics

It is difficult to say anything unpleasant about Mrs. Christie. While she may try to lead you astray, it is in good fun and for the sake of your own entertainment. She never tries to be overly devious, except in the pursuit of a good mystery. And, in fact, most critics of the theater and mystery stories have only good things to say about Agatha Christie.

There have been a few debunkers of the faith. But Agatha Christie, in addition to displaying a large amount of good grace, has outlived everyone and become more of an institution than a mere mortal, subject to the "slings and arrows..."

Years ago, mystery writer Raymond Chandler said that he "couldn't read Christie," but what else could you expect from the hard-boiled creator of Phillip Marlowe. Actually, he proba-

bly secretly read her books, when he wasn't
talking out of the side of his mouth.

Reviews these days may not praise Dame
Agatha's newest works (everyone generally
concedes that she is no longer at the height of
her powers) but they also point out that the re-
doubtable Agatha is, after all, in her eighties,
and we all owe her a great debt of gratitude
for past pleasures. Not to say that all of Agatha Christie's eighty-odd books are greeted
with equal enthusiasm by the critical community. But Christie's best—*The Mysterious Affair at Styles; The Murder of Roger Ackroyd;
Lord Edgeware Dies; Murder on the Orient
Express; The A.B.C. Murders; Cards on the
Table; Ten Little Indians,* and a few more—
generally have been called "great masterpieces
of detective fiction."

But not always. Here is a sample of what
various critics and other mystery writers have
had to say about Mrs. Christie's work over the
years:

On the occasion of Agatha Christie's fiftieth
book, her peer and favorite mystery writer,
Margery Allingham, wrote in the *New York
Times Book Review*:

"As it emerges today the detective story
proper is a form of entertainment almost entirely cerebral, since it aims to provide a means
of escape for those who do not wish for some

excellent private reason to take their emotions for a ride with the novelists. In its never-never land where Death is merely a cipher for the most important happening, and the puzzle is the thing, it is perhaps not at all surprising that a charming, shrewd and essentially civilized matron should be high priestess of the cult."

* * *

"There is no other reality in her tales, nor does the genuine detective story permit any. Grief is out of place here, so is horror, so is fear. These are too near home for the escaping reader in this age of peril. The rest is puzzle, and first-class puzzle, too. To be convincing, the man who says he always guesses an Agatha Christie mystery should also be able to forecast election results and the winners of horse races.

"In her own sphere there is no one to touch her, and her millions of readers are going to buy the new new story, *A Murder is Announced*, and like it."

* * * *

"When her hundredth book is published (on present form this should take place in the fall of '75) she will doubtless receive the 'family canonization' of other minor saints and take her place between Florence Nightingale and Grace Darling."

But in 1926, E.M. Wrong (a name to conjure with), an Oxford professor, wrote: "... Miss Christie's Poirot has twice been mistaken on a point of English law. He thinks that arrest for a crime relieves a man who is discharged of all further risk, and he may find his tasks easier in future if he learns that only trial and acquittal have this result." (This particular point, of course, is the one on which the entire plot twist of *The Mysterious Affair at Styles* is based, and therefore a serious criticism.)

Getting back to the peers of Mrs. Christie, Williard Huntington Wright, a.k.a. S.S. Van Dine, the creator of Philo Vance, said in 1927: "Hercule Poirot, Agatha Christie's pompous little Belgian sleuth, falls in the category of detectival logicians, and though his methods are also intuitional to the point of clairvoyance, he constantly insists that his surprisingly accurate and often miraculous deductions are the inevitable results of the intensive operation of 'the little gray cells.' Poirot is more fantastic and far less credible than his brother criminologists of the syllogistic fraternity. The stories in which he figures are often so artificial, and their problems so far fetched, that all sense of reality is lost, and consequently the interest in the solution is vitiated. This is particularly true of the short stories gathered into the volume *Poirot Investigates*. Poirot is to be seen at his best in *The Mysterious Affair at Styles* and *The Murder on the Links*. The trick played on the reader in *The Murder of Roger Ackroyd* is hardly a legitimate device of the detective-story writer; and while Poirot's work in this book is at times capable, the effect is nullified by the denouement."

The great mystery writer, friend of Mrs. Christie, and creator of the inimitable Lord Peter Wimsey, Dorothy Sayers, answered Van Dine in 1928, saying: "An exceptional handling of the Watson theme is found in Agatha Christie's *Murder of Roger Ackroyd*, which is a *tour de force*. Some critics, as, for instance, Mr. W.H. Wright in his introduction to *The Great Detective Stories* (Scribner's, 1927), consider the solution illegitimate. I fancy, however, that this opinion merely represents a natural resentment at having been ingeniously bamboozled. All the necessary data are given. The reader ought to be able to guess the criminal, if he is sharp enough, and nobody can ask for more than this. It is, after all, the reader's job to keep his wits about him, and, like the perfect detective, to suspect *everybody*."

While there seems to be a certain amount of infighting within the family of mystery writers, an outsider, H. Douglas Thomson, had some basic praise for Mrs. Christie in his 1931 critique of the detective story, *Masters of Mystery*: "So, if the author is as ingenious as Mrs. Agatha Christie, he can play a double game with the reader by establishing a subtle intercommunication between the sheep and the wolves travelling incognito to the forest and the fold."

And back to the family. The aforesaid Raymond Chandler who boasted of his inability to read Mrs. Christie said of her *Murder on the Orient Express* (revealing the dénouement): "... there is a scheme of Agatha Christie's featuring M. Hercule Poirot, that ingenius Belgian who talks in a literal translation of schoolboy French, wherein, by duly messing around with his 'little gray cells,' M. Poirot decides that nobody on a certain through sleeper could have done the murder alone, therefore everybody did it together, breaking the process down into a series of simple operations, like assembling an egg-beater. This is the type that is guaranteed to knock the keenest mind for a loop. Only a halfwit could guess it."

Hercule Poirot is given a good deal more shrift by Ellery Queen (Frederic Dannay and Manfred B. Lee): "That is one of the reasons why Agatha Christie's latest series of Hercule Poirot short stories has a special and unusual appeal. It offers a unity of theme that, unlike the mathematical dictum, is larger than the sum total of the individual parts. Mrs. Christie's literary motif was positively inspired. True, it was made feasible only because the given name of her famous detective is Hercule; but that fortuitous circumstance in no way lessens the brilliance of her basic idea. Isn't Hercule Poirot (Agatha Christie must have asked herself) a modern Hercules? Why not, then, write a sage of modern Herculean labors in which Hercule Poirot emulates his legendary namesake? And so, Poirot, before retiring from active practice (we hope not!), decides to accept only twelve more cases—the Twelve Modern Labors of Hercules.

"Each story stems from an ancient Herculean theme, but the symbolism is completely modernized and detectivized. Thus, in the first "labor" Poirot captures the lion of Nemea—in the modern sense, a kidnaped Pekinese; in the sixth "labor" Poirot deals with the iron-beaked birds of Stymphalus—the modern blackmailers; in the eighth "labor" Poirot tames the wild horses of Diomedes—the modern drug peddlers; and so on.

"If you want an exciting refresher course in mythology, we recommend Agatha Christie's brilliantly conceived *Modern Labors of Hercules*."

Fellow Englishman, pseudonymous mystery writer R. Philmore has this to say about Dame

Agatha's use of motive: "The great classic, *Mysterious Affair at Styles*, is an example of murder for greed. Here Agatha Christie manages by extraordinary clever juggling with clues and devices to hide the lack of clear murderous intent in her main villain. She has tried to do the same thing again, quite often. Perhaps her greatest success in this medium was in *Peril at End House*, where she contrived to create a murderer who, we felt at the end, was probably good for anything: but here the motive was more than greed, it had elements of jealousy and revenge. Here, again, any doubts we may have felt during our next-morning reflection as to the psychological state of the murderer were dispelled by the brilliance of the central detective device."

Philmore also has a reply to Raymond Chandler's words about Poirot in *Murder on the Orient Express*: "The world's horror at kidnapping was capitalized by Agatha Christie in her delightful *Murder on the Orient Express*—a book which, if it is not her best detective story, is certainly Poirot's best and most charming appearance."

Even in her latest, most negative reviews, critics have felt compelled to praise Dame Agatha. While on one hand, they might blast the current book, they always remind us that Agatha Christie is the quintessential writer of the

English mystery and the current work is just not up to her exalted standard. Here is part of such a review by Allen J. Hubin in the *New York Times Book Review*. The book discussed is *Passenger to Frankfurt*, Mrs. Christie's eightieth detective novel.

"Mrs. Christie's popularity remains enormous. She would doubtless head any representative list of women mystery writers, and might well find her way to the top of others embracing the entire field of the novel. And if, in reviewing "Passenger," I'm inclined to dwell on her past performance, it's because the book doesn't really come off; in fact, it doesn't come off at all. This is doubly sad because I suspect Miss Christie has thrown more of herself, of her bewilderment and concern with the present course of humanity, into this book than any other. She has looked upon the current revolt of youth, the preoccupation with violence for its own sake, the pleasure seemingly derived from wholesale destruction. She conjures up a hidden master cause, projects us a few years hence, and creates a band of elderly men to deal with what is by then an international menace. Unfortunately, the whole novel stays one pace removed from real, and the efforts of the benign dodderers verge on the silly."

Dame Agatha usually fares well with the critics of theater. Richard L. Coe, writing in the Washington Post said: " 'The Mousetrap' does indeed fall between comedy and thriller and that's part of its pleasure. As in her score of plays (at one point three were running simultaneously in London), there are insightful details, recognizable characters, quiet humor and a persistent sense of suspense that lasts until the final curtain."

" 'The Mousetrap,' then, is a diversion in the finest sense, satisfying for doing exactly what it aims to do. It is a most successful exercise by a Dame who loves puzzles. Since I never remember who-dun-it and enjoyed this more the third time, that suggests Olney's production is highly superior in its performing genre. So is James D. Waring's set, an exact replica of London's original."

W.A. Darlington, reviewing *Witness for the Prosecution* from London, praised: " 'Witness for the Prosecution' is a big scale whodunit by Agatha Christie, who has a miraculous faculty for constructing puzzles which seem to have one solution and turn out to have another equally plausible. With this she combines an ability to draw characters which actors can play with effect."

And in writing about the same play, famed *New York Times* drama critic Brooks Atkinson wrote, *"Witness for the Prosecution* is one of the best," and bowed to the experts from the mother country, saying, "They order these matters better in England, as Laurence Sterne did not say exactly. In the murder mystery the British are the expert technicians."

From the big productions in the West End of London and on Broadway, to the one-night stands in the hinterlands and Off-Broadway, Dame Agatha is praised by the theater critics. Howard Thompson, writing for the *New York Times*, had only one complaint to make about Christie plays, the criticism that there weren't enough of them around.

If there is one area of her work where Dame Agatha does not intrigue us, it is in her romantic novels written under the name Mary Westmacott. There are six of these, beginning with the 1930 novel, *Giant's Bread*, up to *The Burden*, published in 1956.

Critics have generally treated the Mary Westmacott novels with indifference. And, indeed, if she were a romantic novelist, the world might never have heard of Agatha Christie. But these books, Dame Agatha has remarked, are "not like work at all," and are not considered as part of her serious business—murder.

When it comes to murder, Agatha Christie has few, if any, peers. There is no other writer in history who has dealt with murder and mystery so often and so well. In the long run, it is not the critics who have the say about Dame Agatha's place in history. It is the people—of all tongues, throughout the world—who have bought well on to 400 million of her books. And they have been buying them for more than fifty years.

One of Mrs. Christie's severest critics, S.S. Van Dine, wrote enormously popular mysteries at the same time as the mistress of mystery. Today, Van Dine's books are out of print and seem dated period pieces. The popular works of Ian Fleming will probably go the same way. But Dame Agatha's first book, *The Mysterious Affair at Styles* is more available on the book-racks today than when it was first published. And it is as fresh and entertaining as ever.

Agatha Christie is truly a phenomenon even the critics and her peers have difficulty in pinning down. But Margery Allingham described her well:

"The impression she leaves is that she is a woman of extraordinary ability who could have done anything she chose to do. What she has done is to entertain more people for more hours at a time than almost any other writer of her generation. Taking it by and large, in this day and age it is difficult to think of any work which could possibly have been more useful."

Chapter XII

Agatha Christie Mystery Quiz

1. This scene is from a famous morality tale and helps Tommy and Tuppence solve a five year-old kidnapping.

161

2.   Knowing who wore these and why unravels a particularly thorny mystery for Hercule Poirot. Can you name the book?

3. This man's portrait appeared recently on page one of *The New York Times* (August 6th, 1975). The story, alas, his obituary.

4. A shot was fired and heard at exactly 6:35
P.M., but no one was present. Knowing how
it was done helps Jane Marple solve this be-
guiling mystery tale.

5. What secret did the monstrous hound carry about in his gigantic maw? Hercule Poirot knows at last and roses are a reformed jewel thief's bounty. Can you name the short story collection?

6. ". . . there must be Blackbirds", said Miss
Marple, and knowing who put the clothespin
on the maid's nose brought a triple murderer
to justice in this Christie classic.

7. You must know why there was no sugar in
    the broken tea cup in order to discover, along
    with Hercule Poirot, the murderer's identity.
    Her first novel.

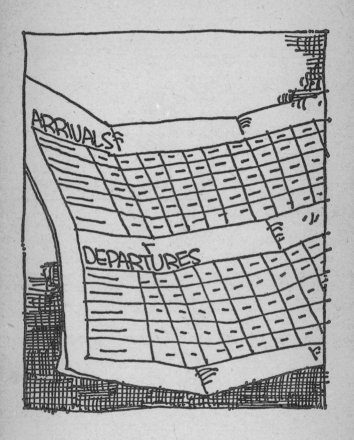

8. The calling card of a murderer—four times—
a famous and much copied mystery.

9. This man makes an extraordinary guaran-
tee—happiness or your money back!

10. This clue led the list that Tuppence compiled, but she had no idea what any of them meant. Can you name the book?

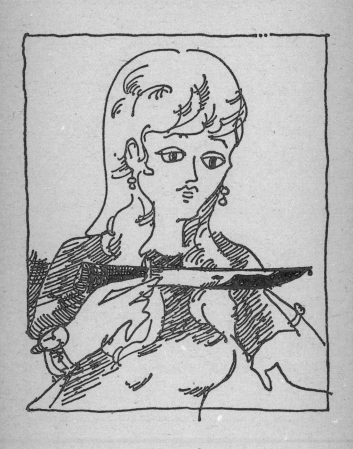

11. She thinks she didn't do it—but why is the
    knife in her hand? Poirot finds out even
    though he is too old for swinging London, in
    this recent Christie mystery.

12.   A disguise for Poirot? Or a detective in his
      own right. He makes the difference in bring-
      ing the murderer to justice in this Christie
      classic.

13. Country houses and estates dot the English countryside, and Dame Agatha has most of them peopled with dead bodies. One dominates two of her thrillers.

14. The shadowy stranger of repellent mien was
fascinating to Anne all the same. He may not
be sartorially resplendent, but his secret
could threaten the Empire. Can you name
the book?

15. Countess or commoner? Jezebel or jewel
     thief? She holds fatal fascination for the
     little Belgian and tells him to go to hell in
     this famous Christie short story. (Turn page
     for answers.)

Answers to Agatha Christie Mystery Quiz:

1. THE SECRET ADVERSARY (1922).

2. LORD EDWARE DIES, or THIRTEEN AT DINNER (1938).

3. HERCULE POIROT

4. MURDER AT THE VICARAGE (1930).

5. THE LABORS OF HERCULES (1947).

6. A POCKET FULL OF RYE (1953).

7. THE MYSTERIOUS AFFAIR AT STYLES (1920).

8. THE A.B.C. MURDERS (1935).

9. PARKER PYNE

10. POSTERN OF FATE (1973).

11. THIRD GIRL (1966).

12. HICKORY, DICKORY, DOCK (1955).

13. THE SECRET OF CHIMNEYS (1925). THE SEVEN DIALS MYSTERY (1929).

14. THE MAN IN THE BROWN SUIT (1924).

15. THE CAPTURE OF CERBERUS (1947).

BIBLIOGRAPHY

The Complete Works of Agatha Christie

THE NOVELS (listed alphabetically):

A.B.C. Murders, The (1935). Features Poirot. Film version (1966) starring Tony Randall under the title *The Alphabet Murders*.

After the Funeral (1953). Features Poirot. Other titles: *Funerals Are Fatal* and *Murder at the Gallop*. Film version, with Miss Marple substituted for Poirot, under the title *Murder at the Gallop*, starring Margaret Rutherford.

Appointment with Death (1938). Features Poirot. Also available in omnibus volume entitled *Make Mine Murder*.

At Bertram's Hotel (1965). Features Miss Marple.

Big Four, The (1927). Features Poirot.

Body in the Library, The (1942). Features Miss Marple.

Cards on the Table (1936). Features Poirot. Also in omnibus volume, *Surprise Endings*.

Caribbean Mystery A (1964). Features Miss Marple.

Cat Among the Pigeons (1959). Features Poirot.

Clocks, The (1963). Features Poirot.

Crooked House (1949).

Curtain (1975). Features Poirot.

Dead Man's Folly (1956). Features Poirot and Ariadne Oliver.

Death Comes as the End (1945).

Death in the Clouds (1935). Features Poirot. American title *Death in the Air*.

Death on the Nile (1937). Features Poirot. Play titled *Murder on the Nile*.

Destination Unknown (1954). American title *So Many Steps to Death*.

Dumb Witness (1937). Features Poirot. Other titles *Poirot Loses a Client. Mystery at Littlegreen House. Murder at Littlegreen House.*

Elephants Can Remember (1972). Features Poirot and Ariadne Oliver.

Endless Night (1967).

Evil Under the Sun (1941). Features Poirot.

Five Little Pigs (1943). Features Poirot. American title *Murder in Retrospect*. Play entitled *Go Back for Murder*.

4:50 from Paddington (1957). Features Miss Marple. Other titles *What Mrs. McGillicuddy Saw!* and *Murder She Said*.

Hercule Poirot's Christmas (1938). Features Poirot. Other titles *Murder for Christmas* and *A Holiday for Murder*.

Hickory, Dickory, Dock (1955). Features Poirot. American title *Hickory, Dickory, Death*.

Hollow, The (1946). Features Poirot. American title *Murder After Hours*. Dramatised by the author (1951) into play entitled *The Hollow*.

Lord Edgware Dies (1938). Features Poirot. American title *Thirteen at Dinner*.

Man in the Brown Suit, The (1924).

Mirror Crack'd from Side to Side, The (1962). Features Miss Marple. American title *The Mirror Crack'd*.

Moving Finger, The (1943). Features Miss Marple.

Mrs. McGinty's Dead (1952). Features Poirot. Another title *Blood Will Tell*. Film version with Miss Marple substituted for Poirot starring Margaret Rutherford, entitled *Murder Most Foul*.

Murder at the Vicarage (1930). Features Miss Marple. Dramatised by Moi Charles and Barbara Toy (1950) into the play of same name.

Murder in Mesopotamia (1936). Features Poirot.

Murder Is Announced, A (1950). Features Miss Marple.

Murder Is Easy (1939). American title *Easy to Kill*.

Murder of Roger Ackroyd, The (1926). Features Poirot. Dramatised by Michael Morton (1928) into play entitled *Alibi*.

Murder on the Links (1923). Features Poirot.

Murder on the Orient Express (1934). Features Poirot. American title *Murder in the Calais Coach*. Film version (1974) titled *Murder on the Orient Express* starring Albert Finney as Hercule Poirot.

Mysterious Affair at Styles, The (1920). Featuring Poirot.

Mystery of the Blue Train (1928). Featuring Poirot. Omnibus volume *Perilous Journeys of Hercule Poirot*.

N or M? (1941). Features Tommy and Tuppence Beresford.

One, Two, Buckle My Shoe (1940). Features Poirot. Other titles *The Patriotic Murders* and *An Overdose of Death*.

Ordeal by Innocence (1958).

Pale Horse, The (1961). Features Mrs. Ariadne Oliver.

Peril at End House (1932). Features Poirot. Dramatised by Arnold Ridley (1940).

Pocket Full of Rye, A (1953). Features Miss Marple.

Postern of Fate (1973). Features Tuppence and Tommy Beresford.

Sad Cypress (1940). Features Poirot.

Secret Adversary, The (1922). Features Tommy and Tuppence Beresford.

Secret of Chimneys, The (1925). Features Superintendent Battle.

Seven Dials Mystery, The (1929).

Sittaford Mystery (1931). American title *Murder at Hazelmoor*.

Sparkling Cyanide (1945). American title *Remembered Death*.

Taken at the Flood (1948). Features Poirot. American title *There Is a Tide*.

Ten Little Niggers (1939). Other titles: *Ten Little Indians, And Then There Were None,*

The Nursery Rhyme Murders. Two film versions: with Barry Fitzgerald and Walter Huston *And Then There Were None*; and with Wilfred Hyde-White and Stanley Holloway *Ten Little Indians.*

They Came to Baghdad (1951).

They Do It with Mirrors (1952). Features Miss Marple. American title *Murder with Mirrors.*

Third Girl (1966). Features Poirot and Ariadne Oliver.

Three-Act Tragedy (1935). Features Poirot. American title *Murder in Three Acts.*

Towards Zero (1944). American title *Come and Be Hanged.* Features Superintendent Battle. Dramatised by Agatha Christie and Gerald Verner (1956).

Why Didn't They Ask Evans (1934). American title *The Boomerang Clue.*

SHORT STORIES (alphabetically listed by collection) :

Adventure of the Christmas Pudding (1960).
Adventure of the Christmas Pudding (Poirot)
Mystery of the Spanish Chest (Poirot)
Under Dog (Poirot)
Four and Twenty Blackbirds (Poirot)
The Dream (Poirot)
Greenshaw's Folly (Miss Marple)

Dead Man's Mirror (1937). Same collection as *Murder in the Mews* plus:

The Incredible Theft
Dead Man's Mirror (Poirot)
Murder in the Mews (Poirot)
Triangle at Rhodes (Poirot)

Double Sin and Other Stories (1961).
Double Sin (Poirot)
Wasps's Nest (Poirot)
Theft of the Royal Ruby (Poirot)
Dressmaker's Doll
Greenshaw's Folly (Miss Marple)
Double Clue (Poirot)
Last Seance
Sanctuary (Miss Marple)

Hound of Death (1933).
Hound of Death
Red Signal
Fourth Man
Gypsy
Lamp
Wireless (another title: Where There's a Will)
Witness for the Prosecution
Mystery of the Blue Jar
Strange Case of Sir Arthur Carmichael
Call of Wings
Last Seance
S O S

Labors of Hercules (1947) (Poirot).
How It all Came About—Foreword
Nemean Lion
Lernean Hydra

Arcadian Deer
Eurymanthian Boar
Augean Stables
Stymphalean Birds
Cretan Bull
Horses of Diomedes
Girdle of Hippolyta
Flock of Geryon
Apples of the Hesperides
Capture of Cerberus

Listerdale Mystery (1934).
Listerdale Mystery
Philomel Cottage
Girl in the Grain
Sing a Song of Sixpence
Manhood of Edward Robinson
Accident
Jane in Search of a Job
A Fruitful Sunday
Mr. Eastwood's Adventure (American title:
Mystery of the Spanish Shawl)
Golden Ball
Rajah's Emerald
Swan Song

Murder in the Mews (1937) (Poirot).
Murder in the Mews
Incredible Theft
Dead Man's Mirror
Triangle at Rhodes

Mysterious Mr. Quin (1930). Another title: *The Passing of Mr. Quin*.

Coming of Mr. Quin
Shadow on the Glass
At the Bells and Motley
Sign in the Sky
Soul of the Croupier
World's End
Voice in the Dark
Face of Helen
Dead Harlequin
Bird with the Broken Wing
Man from the Sea
Harlequin's Lane

Parker Pyne Investigates (1934) (Parker Pyne).

Case of the Middle-Aged Wife
Case of the Discontented Soldier
Case of the Distressed Lady
Case of the Discontented Husband
Case of the City Clerk
Case of the Rich Woman
Have You Got Everything You Want?
The Gate of Baghdad
The House at Shiraz
The Pearl of Price
Death on the Nile (unrelated to novel of same name)
Oracle at Delphi

Partners in Crime (1929) (Tommy and Tuppence Beresford).

A Fairy in the Flat

A Pot of Tea
The Affair of the Pink Pearl
The Affair of the Sinister Stranger
Finessing the King
The Gentleman Dressed in Newspaper
The Case of the Missing Lady
Blindman's Buff
The Man in the Mist
The Crackler
The Sunningdale Mystery
The House of Lurking Death
The Unbreakable Alibi
The Clergyman's Daughter
The Red House
The Ambassador's Boots
The Man Who Was Number 16

Poirot Investigates (1924) (Poirot).
Adventure of the Western Star
Tragedy at Marsdon Manor
Adventure of the Cheap Flat
Mystery of Hunter's Lodge
Million Dollar (Bond) Bank Robbery
Adventure of the Egyptian Tomb
Jewel Robbery at the Grand Metropolitan
Kidnapped Prime Minister
Disappearance of Mr. Davenheim
Adventure of the Italian Nobleman
Case of the Missing Will
Veiled Lady (not published in the English collection)
Lost Mine (not published in the English collection)

Chocolate Box (not published in the English collection)

Regatta Mystery (1939).
  Regatta Mystery (Pyne)
  Mystery of the Baghdad Chest (Poirot)
  How Does Your Garden Grow? (Poirot)
  Problems at Pollensa Bay (Pyne)
  Yellow Iris (Poirot)
  Miss Marple Tells a Story (Miss Marple)
  The Dream (Poirot)
  In a Glass Darkly
  Problems at Sea (Poirot)

Surprise! Surprise! (1965). (Contains no new material)
13 Clues for Miss Marple (1966). (Contains no new material)
13 for Luck (1961). (Contains no new material)
Thirteen Problems (1932). (Miss Marple) American Title *The Tuesday Club Murders*
  Tuesday Night Club
  Idol House of Astarte
  Ingots of Gold
  The Bloodstained Pavement
  Motive versus Opportunity
  Thumb Mark of St. Peter
  Blue Geranium
  Companion
  Four Suspects
  Christmas Tragedy
  Herb of Death

Affair at the Bungalow
Death by Drowning

Three Blind Mice and Other Stories (1950). Also
titled *The Mousetrap and Other Stories*.
Three Blind Mice
Strange Jest
Tape-Measure Murder. Another title Case of
the Retired Jeweller
Case of the Perfect Maid
Case of the Caretaker
The Third Floor Flat
Adventure of Johnny Waverly
Four and Twenty Blackbirds
Love Detectives

Under Dog and Other Stories (1952) (Poirot).
Under Dog
Plymouth Express
Affair at the Victory Ball
Market Basing Mystery
Lemesurier Inheritance
Cornish Mystery
Kong of Clubs
Submarine Plans
Adventure of the Clapham Cook

Witness for the Prosecution and Other Stories
(1948).
Witness for the Prosecution
Red Signal
Fourth Man
S O S

Where There's a Will (English title, Wireless)
Mystery of the Blue Jar
Philomel Cottage
Accident
The Second Gong
Sing a Song of Sixpence

THE PLAYS (listed alphabetically):

Alibi (1928). From the Novel *The Murder of Roger Ackroyd*; dramatised by Michael Morton.

Appointment with Death (1945). From novel of same name; dramatised by Agatha Christie.

Black Coffee (1934). An original play.

Go Back for Murder (1960). From the novel *Five Little Pigs*; dramatised by Agatha Christie.

Hollow, The (1951). From novel of same name; dramatised by Agatha Christie.

Love from a Stranger (1936). From the short story *Philomel Cottage*; dramatised by Agatha Christie and Frank Vosper.

Mousetrap, The (1952). From the short story *Three Blind Mice*. Dramatised by Agatha Christie.

Murder at the Vicarage (1950). From novel of same name; dramatised by Moie Charles and Barbara Toy.

Murder on the Nile (1946). From the novel *Death on the Nile*; dramatised by Agatha Christie.

Peril at End House (1940). From novel of same name; dramatised by Arnold Ridley.

Rule of Three (1962). Three one-act original

plays: *Afternoon at the Seaside, Patient, Rats.*

Spider's Web (1954). An original play.

Ten Little Niggers (1943). From novel of same name; dramatised by Agatha Christie. Also known as *Ten Little Indians;* and *Then There Were None.*

Towards Zero (1956). From novel of same name; dramatised by Agatha Christie and Gerald Verner.

Unexpected Guest (1958). An original play.

Verdict (1958). An original play.

Witness for the Prosecution (1953). Based on short story of same name; dramatised by Agatha Christie.

THE MOVIES (listed Alphabetically):

Alibi—from the play of same name (novel *Murder of Roger Ackroyd.*)

Alphabet Murders - from novel *The A.B.C. Murders.*

Black Coffee - from original play.

Lord Edgware Dies - from novel of same name.

Love from a Stranger - from play of same name (short story *Philomel Cottage*). Filmed twice, second version titled *A Stranger Walked In.*

Murder at the Gallop - from novel *After the Funeral.*

Murder on the Orient Express - 1974 - based on novel of same name.

Murder Most Foul - from novel Mrs. McGinty's Dead.

Murder She Said - from novel *4:50 from Paddington*.

Spider's Web - from original play of same name.

Ten Little Indians - based on play *Ten Little Niggers*. Re-filmed Under same title 1974.

Ten Little Niggers - based on play of same name.
Released in America as *And Then There Were
None*.

Witness for the Prosecution - from play of same
name.

THE PSEUDONYMS

As Mary Westmacott:
   Absent in the Spring (1944).
   Burden, The (1956).
   Daughter's a Daughter (1952).
   Giant's Bread (1930).
   Rose and the Yew Tree (1947).
   Unfinished Portrait (1934).
As Agatha Christie Mallowan:
   Come, Tell Me How You Live (1946).
   Star Over Bethlehem (1965).

FASCINATING, IN-DEPTH PORTRAITS OF JOHN WAYNE, JOHNNY CARSON, JACQUELINE SUSANN AND THE FORD CHILDREN!

HE-E-E-ERE'S JOHNNY
Robert Lardine

Here at last, the inside story of America's number one television personality—Johnny Carson. "Millions of American housewives who've been 'going to bed with Johnny' almost nightly for over twelve years now may wish to examine Mr. Lardine's book the next time Mr. Carson has a substitute host. Well put together!"—**Bestsellers.** Illustrated with pages of intimate photos.

AD1425—$1.50

THE YOUNG FORDS
Jay David

A revealing, behind-the-scenes look at President Ford's children—four unusual young people in the White House who have captured the national spotlight. 16 pages of photos.

AD1416—$1.50

DUKE
Jean Ramer

The real story of John Wayne—from boyhood in Iowa to superstar status as today's biggest film personality. Includes stills and photos.

AQ1185—$1.25

THE JACQUELINE SUSANN STORY
Jeffrey Ventura

The fascinating story of the biggest-selling novelist in history. Each extraordinary chapter reads like one of her runaway best sellers.

AD1482—$1.50

USE HANDY, MONEY-SAVING ORDER FORM ON BACK PAGE

BEST-SELLING NOVELS
FOR PROVEN READING PLEASURE

THE WAKE OF THE RED WITCH   Garland Roark

The splendid color and savagery of the South Pacific adds to the sweeping scope of this novel of courage, romance and fabulous lost treasure. "A stunning adventure saga of the sea . . . overflowing with brutal passion and suspense."—Hampton Press.   AD1138—$1.50

THE MUSCOVITE   Alison Macleod

A superbly crafted novel of 16th-century adventure and intrigue, from the barbaric splendor of Moscow to the dazzling elegance of the European capitals.   AD1269—$1.50

CITY OF LIGHT   Alison Macleod

"Miss Macleod tells a whopping good story in this continuation of the Tudor-age adventures of Thomas Vaughan."—Kirkus Reviews. "An exciting tale of adventure, authentic and believable."—Publishers Weekly.   AD1295—$1.50

RUSH YOUR ORDER TODAY!

AWARD BOOKS, 350 Kennedy Drive,
Hauppauge, N.Y. 11788

Please send me the books checked below by number:

☐ AD1425	$1.50	☐ AD1138	$1.50
☐ AD1416	$1.50	☐ AD1269	$1.50
☐ AQ1185	$1.25	☐ AD1295	$1.50
☐ AD1482	$1.50		

I am enclosing $_____.

SAVE $ $ $ 5 books or more, deduct 10% discount
DISCOUNT   8 books or more, deduct 15% discount
PLAN   10 books or more, deduct 20% discount

Name_____

Address_____

City_____ State_____ Zip_____

Add 25¢ for postage and handling for one book, 35¢ for two or three books. We pay postage on all orders of four books or more. Send remittance in U.S. or Canadian funds. Sorry, no C.O.D.s.